CW00684778

ISBN 978-0-9557258-2-1
Printed by PMM Group (UK) Ltd – 01423 810 111

Third Edition 2011

Foreword

Keats, Wordsworth, Byron. Just three of the poets currently spinning in their graves at the mere mention of Doris and Elsie.

Of course we all know that these two venerable ladies are probably older than the aforementioned gents, but did we also know that they were better than them too!

Well hang on and I'll try to persuade you.

Did Keats ever consider dyeing his hair red to match a Ferrari?

Did Wordsworth while bathing ever contemplate rhyming the dirty ring around the rim with Vim?

And I know for a fact that Phillip Larkin would rather have found a rhyme for orange than spend a weekend in a Fleetwood B and B with Bert and Len.

The other thing that Doris and Elsie have done that these unimaginative if legendary poets weren't as eager to do is raise thousands of pounds for Derian House Children's Hospice in and around Lancashire. So well done for buying this book and supporting our favourite ladies.
Tony Livesey

"Doris and Elsie, can be compared to a fine Lancashire Hotpot, full bodied, you just can't get enough of them."
Alec Makinson

"Doris and Elsie, there's just no rhyme nor reason for them."
Alison Butterworth

Contents

For never failing to laugh

we dedicate this book
to
Carole Turner
along with all the friends we
make when we go out and about,
your laughter and generosity make it
all worthwhile.

"Laughter is the shortest distance between two people"
Victor Borge 1909-2000

Acknowledgements

This re-print of 'The Best of Doris and Elsie' came about because we still keep being asked for it, so we decided to add a bit more content and go for a second edition

As ever we would like to say a big thank to all the wonderful people who have helped with all the Doris and Elsie books without whose kind support they would have never been printed. Our sincere thanks go to the following.

Our friend Linda Sawley, one the busiest people we know; a very talented author in her own right and still she finds time to help us. Linda you're a star.

Jim Bowen and Sally Naden, we've said it before but if it hadn't been for you two there wouldn't have been any Doris and Elsie books.

Bernard Wrigley who always finds time for us, Bernard we just wish our books could be as funny as yours.

All our friends at BBC Radio Lancashire; your help has been invaluable.

Martin Pendlebury our illustrator, yet again you've come up with some cracking cartoons, but Martin is this really how you see us?

Reg Whittam at The Garth Dawson Studio in Accrington has donated his time and expertise yet again and by some miracle has managed to make us look around 55 plus V.A.T. Reg, you're a gentleman and a true professional!

But as ever the biggest vote of thanks goes to all the wonderful people out there who buy our books or book us to do a 'turn.' With your help we have been able to give Derian House Children's Hospice around £3000 to date and as ever we shall continue to give fifty pence of every book we sell to our chosen charity.

Anne Wareing and Kath Eccleston

Introduction

Welcome to the wonderful world of Doris Rawbottom and Elsie Arkwright, two feisty Lancashire housewives, who have had the misfortune to be married for far too many years to Bert and Leonard.

Doris and Elsie have worked hard all their married lives and are now semi retired.

Bert and Leonard, have worked as little as possible during *their* married lives and are now completely and utterly retired from any kind of exertion what so ever.

Doris and Elsie have remained completely faithful to Bert and Leonard, except that is for the odd flirtation of Doris's.

Bert and Leonard on the other hand have remained completely unfaithful, her at Number four proving to be a constant temptation to both of them.

Doris and Elsie are the original cock eyed optimists, things can only get better.

Bert and Leonard on the other hand view life through the wires of the ferret's cage and the bottom of a pint glass.

Doris and Elsie…. Well, why don't you just read on…………?

CLOSE ENCOUNTERS
OF THE FATAL KIND

Cross Bars and Perfect DA's
Her at Number Four

CROSSBARS AND PERFECT DA'S

Marriage you can keep it
We wouldn't do it again
But I'll tell you how me and Doris
Met our Bert and Len

Valentine Dance, Tony's Ballroom
Both of us dressed up to the nine
Three starched petticoats, waspie belts
We did have waists at one time

We were on the floor dancing together
We'd both been learning to bop
I spotted this lad with a perfect DA
And there's *my* beehive starting to flop

I fair fancied his teddy boy outfit
Brothel creepers, knotted string tie
'Is he looking?' I said to Doris,
She said. 'Stop trying to catch his eye'

Then him and his mate sauntered over
'Do either of you fancy a dance?'
'I do' I said and grabbed his arm
Before Doris got a chance

Said his name were Bert Arkwright
Worked on British Rail
And did I know me hair were falling down
Flattery it never fails

So Doris were left with t'other
Tweed jacket, brylcreemed hair
Brown leather brogues and glasses,
She mouthed. 'It just isn't fair'

We bopped to Bill Haley and the Comets
I danced 'til I were red in the face
I could see Doris doing a fair hand jive
Tweed jacket trying to keep pace

Bert asked. 'Do you fancy a cooling drink
I said. ' I'll have a cherry B'
He said he'd have a pint and a chaser
But he'd lost his wallet you see

Doris had managed to get rid of hers
Said with some chaps you can never tell
Not a pleasant experience, she needed a drink
So I had to buy hers as well

11'oclock came, time to go home
Bert said he'd give me a lift
I said to him. 'But we can't leave Doris
Look at her face, it's all miffed'

'Well I expect I'll have to manage
I just hope it's not too far
But I must say you're both quite hefty
To fit on one crossbar'

We managed to cling on together
Bert perched on saddle at back
We were scuttering round this corner
When crossbar gave an almighty crack

We laid there dazed on the cobbles
A voice said. 'Bert, are you at it again
You're never satisfied wi' just one bird
And by the way I'm his best mate Len'

He picked us up and dusted us off
And they said they'd walk us home
Four miles in winkle pickers is no mean feat
We'd have been better on last bus, alone

So that's how me and Doris got lumbered
Valentines night, both of us footsore
And who gets a lift on their crossbar now
Yes! You've guessed it, number four

No, marriage hasn't been easy
But we promised for better or worse
That's what you get, falling for perfect DA's
Your heart broken and an empty purse

HER AT NO 4

We've decided to go on a diet
'Cos we've both had a bit of a fright
We'd got a bit complacent
Thinking we looked alright

It started a week last Tuesday
A visit from her at number 4
Bert went to answer the knocker
And there's a stick insect stood at the door

She'd come for a cup of sugar
How's that for an original excuse
Said Doris, with that look in her eye
'That women, she's out on the loose'

'Calling round on some pretext
She's well known as a fast little flirt
With her rouged cheeks, lipstick and powder
Fluttering false eyelashes at Leonard and Bert'

You could see they were all of a quiver
They fair seemed to get in a state
And when she left with the sugar
Fell over themselves to open the gate

Well now they've taken to having their hair done
And going round dressed in their best
But the biggest surprise of all is
They're changing their underpants and vest

They're making an almighty effort
To spruce up and try and look neat
And believe us for them two lazy things
It really is quite a feat

Well Doris is upset, I can tell you
Even though Leonard's not much of a catch
With his beer belly and bad habits
And that irritating itch and scratch

But as to her stealing Bert Arkwright
I don't think he'll go far astray
She'll never prise him away front a telly
He's usually stuck there all day

But apparently they're not the first ones
There's been so many she's lost track
I can tell you though, we weren't right pleased
'Cos the sugar didn't come back

So we're just going to have to watch 'em
Anyroad she's far to thin
Just maybe we should stick to the diet
Me and Doris, and get in trim

DESPERATE MEASURES

Purple Curls and Leather Pants
Heavenly Bodies
White Lycra and Chippy Teas
Grapevines and Arrows

PURPLE CURLS AND LEATHER PANT'S

I said to Doris last weekend
'Eee love your hair's a mess
If I were you I'd get it done
'Ave it nice for when you wear
your new dress'

'There's a new place down the precinct
They say he's come from Gay Paree'
'Right'she said, 'He'll do for us
Let's catch bus down and we'll see'

We stood and stared, *Pierre Coiffure*
It were all black windows and chrome
Tight leather trousers and mini skirts
I'm glad we left them two at home

A voice said,
"Are you collecting for Age Concern?'
She'd spiked green hair, a ring in her nose
'Can we have two trims, shampoo and set'?
'Oh no – we don't do those!'

'Well what do you do?'asked Doris
'Just get us this Pierre'
'Allo Mesdames – we don't do ze sets
Mais oui – I can improve your 'air'

'Vous two will be a challenge
Vous will put my art to the test'
And fingering Doris's hair he said
'Zis looks like ze birds nest'

I whispered, 'He's no foreigner Doris
Though it says he's coiffered in Monmatre
That's an Oswaldtwistle accent
Mind you, he certainly looks the part'

We're used to leaning over kitchen sink
With a jug to swill off shampoo
And when they said sit down here
We lent over as you do

She looked as us and tutted
'This is a back wash, can't you see?'
I said, 'We don't need one, we were up early
We'd a bath this morning, Doris and me'

Anyroad before you could say Eiffel Tower
We were shampooed in this tipped up chair
He covered me in pieces of kitchen foil
And Doris had blue gunge on her hair

He kept flitting between the two of us
Leather pants – well they were stretched
to the limit
Doris whispered, 'I think they call it a lunchbox
But there's not much room for 'owt in it'

When he'd finished we stood at reception
Spiky hair, chewed gum and gazed round
'Well you both look ten years younger' she said
'And for both of you it's £80'

We caught our reflections in window
On top deck going home
£80 and look at state of us
Can I borrow your comb

Goodness knows what Bert and Len'll think
'Well' said Doris, 'Let's go in and we'll soon see
They were watching tele –
but they both glanced up
Then Bert said, 'What you making for tea?'

HEAVENLY BODIES

We've been slimming nigh on twenty years
Since we were both about thirty five
But fat still hovers round the girth
And lingers on our thighs

We've tried just about every diet
And stayed on them for at least a week
We've done press-ups, sometimes
five at a time
'Til Bert and Len can here our bones creak

We've tried to keep fit all our lives
Regularly, at least twice a year
We do aerobics, swimming and yoga
But we don't overdo it, no fear

Have you been on them toning tables?
Your bodies up and down in a trice
Doris got all hot and bothered
She said, 'It doesn't seem nice'

'One leg's down, whilst the other is up
I can't say I'm having fun
And I shouldn't of come in this tight skirt
I should have put some leggings on'

We did quite well on the F Plan
All that roughage and baked beans
But it's hardly user friendly
When you spend half the day in t'latreens

Then we tried that food combining
But it were ever so confusing
So we ate everything together at one go
But we still didn't seem to be loosing

Well Doris came up with a new one
A diet something to do with Hay
I said, 'Well I'm not eating grass
Last thing I want to do, is neigh'

We tried a small bowl of muesli for breakfast
Then salad for dinner and tea
But we'd to have fish, chips and
mushies for supper
Can't sleep on empty stomachs you see

Anyroad we bought a tin of powder
To make this strawberry drink
Supposed to fill you up and taste quite nice
But it were such a lurid pink

But we didn't want to throw it away
We don't like waste at all
So we got two brushes and a roller
And painted t' back yard wall

What is it with men and skinny women?
We reckon it's all this show biz
Magazines and Sunday supplements
They don't know what a real woman is

Anyway we don't want to get too thin
We've enough lines as it is
So from now on no more dieting
I think we'll give it a miss

'Cos we're both quite happy
with the way we are
We're certainly not exercising for hours
It's taken a lot of money and chocolate
To get bodies as cuddly as ours

WHITE LYCRA AND CHIPPY TEAS

We went away last weekend
We won this competition you see
Two tickets for a luxury health farm
Well we need it – Doris and me

We arrived 9 o'clock Saturday morning
It were just like a grand stately home
What a treat to get away from them two
When all they ever do is moan

A young lady met us in reception
All in white, an obvious size ten
Doris asked. 'Are they all like you,
who work here?'
'Oh no' she said. 'There's one or two men'

We unpacked and put on our tracksuits
Looking forward to our new found hobby
Doris in Bert's old Adidas
Looked like a blue Mrs. Blobby

We met in reception for a pep talk
Size 10 stood with clipboard in hand
She said. 'Ladies, no booze,
cake or chocolates
And welcome to our happy little band'

There were loads of activities on offer
We ticked the ones we thought we might do
And sipping a glass of fresh carrot juice
Read this poster that said, '*A New You*'

We were taken down to the Steam Room
This man said. 'Hi, I'm Julian the masseur
Right ladies, take your clothes off'
I said. 'Doris, I'm not so sure'

She said, 'Come on, let's have a sauna'
But we couldn't see a thing through smoke
We fumbled our way through the bodies
And got a shock when one were a bloke

Well we managed to stay in five minutes
Then gasping for breath ran for pool
I said. 'Doris did you see what I'd hold of
I felt such a blooming fool'

We did a couple of widths doing breaststroke
Then famished we went in for dinner
But there were only grapefruit on offer
Still we wanted to look ten pounds thinner

In afternoon there were a body wrap
and facial
But cling film weren't quite wide enough
So they covered us up with a fluffy white towel
While size 10 gave us faces a buff

Then Julian appeared in white lycra
Saying. 'Right ladies, it's time for your rub'
He dribbled scented oil all over us
Doris said. 'I prefer this to going down pub'

Well after being massaged and pummeled
It were time to make our way home
They put us on scales before leaving
And between us we'd lost half a stone

Their faces when we got home were a picture
They expected new women, you see
I said. 'Don't stand there gawping you two
Go and get us a chippy for t'tea'

GRAPEVINES AND ARROWS

She stood there looking sheepish
Shivering in her vest
'Doris' I said. 'What have you done?'
I tell you, I'd never have guessed

Talk about mid-life crises
And she gets the pension you know
I said. 'What on earth were you thinking of
You can *never* put it on show'

'I don't see why not Elsie
I've heard *she's* done it at number four'
I said. 'She might have, but she's a slapper
What have you gone and done it for?'

'Well there's a new place down the precinct
This young fella were stood outside
'Good morning young lady he sez to me
Would you like to look inside?'

'He were tall and tanned and handsome
Said it were all the rage
All the pop stars are doing it
And besides I didn't look me age'

'Said he'd be ever so gentle
And to make myself comfy on't bed
Only took cash and gold cards'
'So he didn't half con you' I said

'He asked me where did I want it'
I said. 'Well, what do you suggest?'
'Well it's a case of where I can do it
A patch of *smooth* skin is the best'

'Would I like the name of a loved one?'
'I do all sorts of flowers and heart shapes'
'I told him I were fond of a drop of wine
So I'd have a vine and some grapes'

'Talk about bite on a bullet
But I didn't make a sound
I tell you it fair brought tears to my eyes
When he charged me £60'

'Well you'd better show me quick' I said
'Before your Len gets back
That grapevine looks lopsided to me
Or maybe its your skin that's slack'

'Eh up! we've got a visitor
Quick pull your ganzie down'
'You don't need to bother I saw you' she said
'Going in Tattoo Parlour up town'

'So it's a bunch of grapes and vine leaves!
When your Len clocks it he'll go bananas
Mind you with wrinkly skin like yours
They look more like sultanas'

She leant over chair back and folded her arms
Saying 'Do *you* like mine?' The tart
And peeping above her low scooped top
Was an arrow piercing a heart

'And whose name's written on that?' I asked
Sarcastically with a frown
'That's for me to know and you to find out
He did names further down'

SPARE TIME ACTIVITIES

Authentic Kit and Dubious Males
Spreading the Sheets
Green Eyed Cha Cha Cha
Umbrellas and Fish Heads
Backyards and Fig Leaves

AUTHENTIC KIT AND DUBIOUS MALES

Taster sessions they call 'em
Down at Age Concern
Mind you me and Doris aren't old enough
But there's always summat to learn

As you know Bert and Len have football
And racing and gambling are rife
Then there's fishing and her at No 4
All featuring heavily in their life

So we went down to the centre
To see just what they had
On offer, 'cos *we* need a hobby
Summat that won't be a fad

There were keep fit, art and pottery
Flower arranging, cookery perchance
Then we spotted this 'ere poster
Mondays, come and learn to Belly Dance

'That should suit us,' said Doris
'The main ingredient we've got
Big and round and wobbly
All you do is shake it a lot'

We enquired about the costumes
When we went down to enroll
You need floaty scarves and a beaded bra
And very little else at all

So Saturday we went down t'market
Bought a load of beads
Sequins and a bit o'netting
I said. 'I reckon that's all we need'

We spent the weekend stitching
It needed plenty of beads on the bust
We decided not to show Bert and Len
Didn't want to inflame their lust

Monday we walked down to the centre
It isn't very far
We were just changing into our costumes
I said. 'Through window, isn't that your car?'

And there were Robin Reliant
Guess who were climbing out
Bert and Len in attendance
Her, wearing practically nowt

'What's *she* doing here?' I said 'Doris'
'Eee love, you don't half look mift'
She said. 'Well, where ever we go
too she turns up
And them two giving her a lift'

'Eh up! don't let her see us' I said
'Quick pull up your veil'
'Right ladies' the dance teacher shouted
'Are your ready to shake your tail?'

Number 4 were trying her hardest
But couldn't keep up with Doris and me
She looked like a stick insect doing the twist
She's very little to wobble you see

Then teacher remarked. 'You two are naturals
You've certainly let yourselves go'
Well that's a bit rude' I replied to her
She said. 'No, I want you for a show'

'Can I be in it as well' said a voice
'Look I've got the authentic kit'
I said. 'I think it's time to reveal ourselves
And watch *her* have a fit'

'I can't believe it's you two' she cried
I said. 'We saw you with Bert and Len
And if our kit looked as flat as yours
We'd not be belly dancing again'

So now we've got quite a following
Well, there's one or two dubious males
But we always keep our vests on
And cover wobbly bits with veils.

SPREADING THE SHEETS

It was a week last Sunday morning
When Doris went off the rails
We were having a look round
this trading estate
When she spotted a computer Sale

'Come on,' she said 'Let's look around
It's time we got up to date
We need to enter the IT race
Before it gets too late'

Well I weren't so sure, but she forged ahead
Up and down the aisles. She said
'I reckon they're better than typewriters
And oh look, you can have free trials'

'Can I help you madame'
I heard this deep voice say
'Personal installation can be arranged
I can come round any day'

'I can teach you how to E mail
Do letters and spreadsheets'
I could tell by the look on Doris's face
He'd swept her off her feet

He stood there in his dark blue suit
White shirt – blue spotted tie
He smiled at Doris, flashed white teeth
And gazed into her eye

'I'll take one now,' said Doris
'Delivery, how long will it tek?'
'Doris,' I said. 'I'd think about it'
'Too late, I'm signing the cheque'

'We'll bring it pm next Tuesday'
I said, 'What's your Len going to say?'
'It'll be a nice surprise for him,' she said
'When he comes back, he's out for the day'

I were hot and bothered when we got outside
'Doris what have you done?'
'Got up to date, that's what,' she said
'It's time I had some fun'

She her nails done, hair set and a facial
She said. 'I want to look me best'
Eyebrows, new perfume a
pair of high heels
And a brand new lacy look vest

Tuesday morning bright and early
Doris were up at the crack
Packed Len's butties and sent him off
'You don't need to be early back'

Middle of th'afternoon a van turned up
Doris stood there, poised at front door
See through negligee, vest underneath
I'd not seen her like this before

'Where do you want it missus?' he said
Brown overall, cap on t'head
'Where's that nice young man?' Doris asked
'And I were having it next to bed'

'He's back at store busy selling
Deliveries? No he hasn't the time'
She said, 'He said he'd help me to
spread the sheets'
He said, 'He will do, but you ring the help line'

Poor thing were ever so downhearted
I said, 'See, you should leave men alone
It's cost a fortune, now you're stuck with it
So you might as well get on that phone'

We soon got it fixed up and running
Now she's a dab hand at surfing the net
And as to a bit of the other
Well I reckon that's as close as she'll get

THE GREEN EYED CHA CHA CHA

One, two, Cha Cha Cha
Left foot forward, two three four
I can see Doris puffing and blowing
T'other side o' ballroom floor

We've come to Royal Dance Club
We decided we'd like to learn
To do the jive and Cha Cha
'Cos we've a few calories to burn

We're keeping these lessons a secret
We've not told Bert and Len
After their performance at
Christmas do
We don't want showing up again

They spent the night dancing with her
Course she knows all the right moves
Thinks she can drive our husbands wild
Well, me and Doris are getting in t'groove

It's no fun being a wallflower
We never get asked to dance
So we thought maybe we could
learn to gyrate
Then we might just stand a chance

Dance instructor were tanned
and handsome
But honestly, I've got to say
He were clutching Doris round middle
In a most unseemly way

'I'm sorry, Mrs Rawbottom' he said
'But my arm just won't go round
I'll have to hang on to back of your frock
Let's hope we don't crash to ground'

All t'other men were spoken for
I'd to dance with this women called Nellie
She'd blue spiky hair, a ring in her nose
And another one in her belly

There were mirrored balls on t'ceiling
And ultra violet light
It were sort 'a dark and a bit romantic
But it showed up me dandruff all right

Three, four, Cha Cha Cha
Doris's face were going bright red
'I feel like I'm fighting with a sack a' coal
And losing' her partner said

He twirled her round a couple of times
She tripped and pulled him to floor
And as they lay there on the deck
Guess who came through door?

He were stood there glowering,
cap in hand
Someone had tipped off her Len
'Put that young man down
we're going home
You'll not be coming again'

Mind you, Doris is right suited
Times Len's bin jealous aren't very many
And she reckons lessons at
Royal Dance Club
Are worth every bloomin' penny

UMBRELLAS AND FISH HEADS

Our two have started fishing
Getting up at crack o'dawn
It's good to have 'em out 'a house
All they ever do is moan

Their maggots are in a tub in fridge
Tackle's hung up in t'hall
And when they're not down on canal bank
They practice casting o'er back yard wall

They warm their maggots in their mouth
Before they put 'em on line
It seems to be doing trick all right
They catch big 'uns from time to time

Bert came home with a 12 pounder
Said he'd struggled to get it ashore
I tell you it were a good 10 inches
We've not seen one that big before'

Now there's a fair bit of fish in our freezer
Salmon, trout, a heck of a lot
Bert said, 'don't worry we can sell some
And profit can go into pot

Sometime they do some night fishing
Reckon then, they're easier to catch
They've jackets with huge inside pockets
And enormous green waders to match

Now last Tuesday were lovely and sunny
Number four's door hadn't opened all day
In fact we haven't seen much of her lately
I said, 'Let's go round and say'

'Did she fancy coming with us
Down canal to see them two'
We knocked loudly, but no answer
So we went on our own, as you do

We'd a pleasant stroll down towpath
Sun were lovely and hot
'I wonder what they've caught?' I said
'We'll soon see what they've got'

'Elsie, isn't that their umbrella?'
She said, 'I expect they're having a nod'
'But there's three pair of legs poking out
Elsie, she's hold of his rod!!'

Scrambling out came Bert and Len
Faces all guilty and hot
Then *she* crawled out backwards way
Wearing? Well not a lot

Well I tell you we'd just about had enough
Me and Elsie suddenly saw red
I clouted her hard with me handbag
Right on her silly blonde head

Between us we tipped her in water
I tell you she fair weighed a bit
'And since she's an expert with your rod
You'd better fish her out with it,

Well they fell over each other
trying to help her
About to administer kiss of life
I said, 'Don't you dare go near her
It's me you should kiss, I'm your wife'

They said they had to check their tackle
So back under brolly they went
We could hear 'em talking about flies
And how Bert's rod had got bent

So after much cursing and swearing
We decideded to make our way back
Only to find soggy slapper
Squelching along on the track

They hadn't much to show for a days fishing
Far too much botherin' if you ask me
So they can cook for themselves tonight
Me and Elsie are going out for us tea

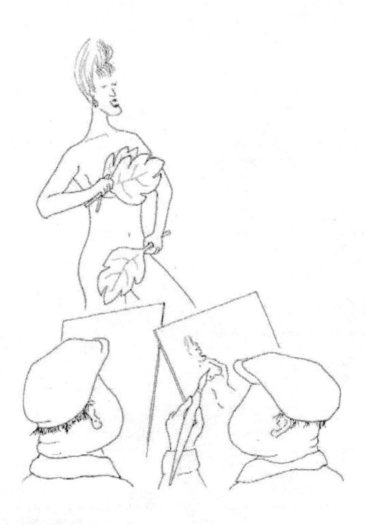

BACKYARDS AND FIG LEAVES

Now Bert and Len never do much
'Cept sit in front o'telly
Read Sporting Life, then fall asleep
Hands clasped on their beer belly

So it came as some surprise to us
When they said they'd got an idea
Bert said. 'Evening classes would benefit us
Especially this time of year'

'Spring-time in the garden,' Len agreed
There's always a lot to do
Let's go on Thursday to night school
We could pick up a tip or two'

'Doris,' I said. 'Can you believe your ears?
It's usually left to you and me
Only gardening I've ever seen them two do
Is watch Charlie Dimmock on TV'

Anyroad we reckon our backyards
are in for a treat
Wi' plants and shrubs re-arranged
But they've been going to these classes four
weeks now
And nothing much has changed

'Doris,' I said. 'We've to encourage them
And I don't like to make a complaint
But have you noticed when they get back
Their hands are covered in paint?'

'I've a funny feeling about it
I just don't trust them two
Next Thursday will nip down to night school
And investigate, me and you'

Well Thursday came and off they went
We followed 'em, half hour behind
We asked at reception where gardening
class were
Wondering what we would find

'Gardening's Mondays,' receptionist said
'Thursday's, macramé, sewing and art
If you fancy joining, go to room 19
Drawing from life, is about to start'

And there they both were, at front o'class
Sat at easels, paint up their sleeves
And guess who were model for life class
With three fig leaves and an apple, like Eve?

'Cover yourself up woman,' screamed Doris
'You brazen hussy, without your vest'
I said. 'Look at her Doris,
she's all skin and bone
Not like us two Ruben-esque'

Well we got 'em back home, read the riot act
And backyard? Well there's no change there
But we've heard they need models and
it's £10 an hour
So we're wondering which one of us dares.

BALLS AND BIKES

Bowling with Jack
Vicars and Cricket Balls
Emails and Old Bicycles
In a League of her Own

BOWLING WITH JACK

We thought we might try this bowling thing
But everyone kept mentioning Jack
We believe its all running and bending
Not good when you've got a bad back

And then of course there's the clothing
It's skirts and blouses, pure white
But Bert rubs his bowls on his trousers
To get them clean, takes us all night

We just can't get to grip with the rules
Though we watched a few matches last year
It seems you roll a bowl across the grass
Then run to try and beat it, oh dear

But we thought we'd try and have a go
So we picked up one of the bowls
Turned it over and over in our hands
But still couldn't find the holes

We couldn't see skittles or an alley
And Doris were having a struggle to bend
Someone shouted, '*Aim for Jack*'
But he were sat at t'other end

So we decided to have a nice pot of tea
But the scones were burnt to a cinda
We'd just chosen a table to watch the game
When Jack came flying through winda

'Pick up your bowls' we heard 'em shout
'Somebody's not playing right
Those two women sat in tea bar
It hasn't half give 'em a fright'

'Is there a doctor in the house?
They're both clean out on t'floor
Well at least it's shut the pair of them up
We should have thrown Jack, before'

It took us both a bit to come round
Doris said, 'Eee me head feels mazy
I said, 'I've had enough of this
Flying Jacks, this game's crazy'

Thank goodness for the St. John Ambulance
We were both taken home in style
You can keep your Crown Green Bowling
We'll not be coming back for a while

VICARS AND CRICKET BALLS

Here we all are sat in t'hospital
Bert, Doris Leonard and me
All because vicar asked us
If we could manage to do cricket tea

There were a knock on t'door last Saturday
And vicar were standing there
I said. 'Come in won't you reverend
Why don't you sit down in that chair?'

Bert and Len were watching racing
And they both looked up in alarm
We saw 'em trying to hide their beer
Down by side of chair arm

He said. 'I'm glad I've caught you 'together
I've got a favour to ask
We're playing St Chad's at cricket next week
And cricket teas are proving a task'

'So I thought you two ladies might fit the bill
I can get you some help from the choir
And if you're doing nothing Leonard and Bert
One could be scorer and t'other th'umpire'

Well we both want to go to heaven
Being married certainly been hell
I said. 'Doris, me and Bert'll do it
And you and Len'll do it as well'

Day dawned bright and sunny
We'd ordered food well in advance
I said. 'Doris we'll have to watch that choir
Or they'll lead us a merry old dance'

Bert were practicing raising one finger
Stood there dressed all in white
Only trouble, jacket, fit where it touched
He didn't half look a sight

Len were stuck up in this box
He were supposed to put up the score
'It won't be accurate,' I could hear him shout
'I'm missing numbers five and four'

Vicar went in first to bat
Crowd roared. 'Come on St Chad's'
I didn't like the look of their bowler
And rest of team were rough lads

He stood manly at t' wicket, with gritted teeth
Bat square on t'line he'd med
Bowler let fly, he hit ball hard
And it landed on th'umpires head

They carried him off on an old backdoor
We put it straight in back of our car
Then me Doris and Len squeezed in the front
At least t' hospital weren't very far

A pretty young nurse took him in hand
He came round and well, he started to flirt
I said. 'Doris, there's not much wrong with him now
He never gives up, does my Bert'

She said. 'Well he seems to be alright
But he's a bit of a bump, I can see
Why did he have to get in t'way of ball?
We've all gone and missed cricket tea'

So next time vicar comes calling
We've decided we're going to say no
And as for heaven, well if them two are going
Me an Doris don't want to go

EMAILS AND OLD BICYCLES

'He's eating us out of house and home
Our Nellie's grandson Wayne
He landed on Saturday with his mountain bike
And some sort of plug in game'

'Says it's called a play-station
And it's time we got up to date
He's never been off Bert's computer
Stopping up ever so late'

'I tell you Doris I keep telling him off
But he always answers back
Except when I'm shouting of him to get up
He seems to go deaf in the sack'

'Mind you I've got to admit it
He has been encouraging Bert
To take a bit of exercise
And that certainly not going to hurt'

'He's borrowed an old bicycle
And he's off with Wayne for a ride
Seems he's never in these days
Traveling far and wide'

'Funny you should say that Elsie
My Len's been at it as well
Dug his old bike out'a garden shed
I tell you, you never can tell'

'Eh up Doris, here comes Wayne
Where's your Uncle Bert?'
'Well we'd gone for a ride down by cut
When he suddenly put on a spurt'

'Pedaled like mad round these bushes
Going like what for
And that woman on her bike were behind 'em
I think she lives at number four'

'Then all of a sudden Uncle Len turned up
Seemed surprised to see me, but
Said they'd give me a fiver and a
couple of fags
If I agreed to keep my trap shut'

'Well you haven't, have you?' said Doris
'So you can give me that fiver right now
And the ciggies can go in the dustbin
There's going to be a row'

Wayne said. 'There's other things I can tell you
If I can I have my fiver back?'
'Well it'd better be worth it' said Doris
'It is, how's this for the crack?'

'You know Uncle Bert's computer
Well do you know what an email is?
They get messages from their girlfriend
And she always signs off with a kiss'

'And sometimes she mentions you two
Says you're battleaxes, frumpy and old
Making Uncle Bert and Len's lives a misery
And she says they shouldn't do as they're told'

Well, our Wayne went back home
with his fiver
His tales, it were proved were well founded
So the plug's been pulled on Bert's computer
And their bicycles they've been grounded

IN A LEAGUE OF HER OWN

They've been going to Fraser Eagle Stadium
On a Saturday afternoon
Bert says they're doing well you know
Be top o' the league very soon

Saturdays we go down market
Have a look round at stalls
Then go and have a pot of tea
You get a good brew in t'Market Hall

Now afternoon were lovely and sunny
Bert and Len had gone to watch game
Doris said. 'It's a pity to miss this sunshine
Why don't us two do the same?'

'It'll do us good to get some fresh air
And it won't half surprise our two
There's a shop there for supporters
We'll get a scarf and hat, me and you'

'Is there a reduction for ladies?'
I asked this fella on the gate
'You don't look like ladies to me' he said
'But I'll do you pensioner rate'

'Cheeky monkey,' I retorted
'Is this what football's all about?'
'Make sure you cheer for home side,' he said
'I reckon Stanley'll hear you two shout'.

It were a tight fit going through turnstile
I'd to shove poor Doris through
She said she'd got wedged with her handbag
But it were her rear end, between me and you

We nipped in shop, bought wooly hats
and scarves
We do look good in red
Doris tied her scarf in a floppy bow
Matching bobble hat on her head

We'd just sat down on second row
And were trying to spot Bert and Len
When two teams of fellas ran onto field
I tell you they were fit young men

'Doris,' I said, 'he's familiar
Him in green top stood in goal
Isn't it your Ethel's grandson
Don't they call him Paul?'

We followed game as best we could
We know nowt about football
There were an almighty scuffle
round goalmouth
Centre forward dived on our Paul

Doris leapt over the barrier
Swinging her handbag round
As ref blew whistle, Paul kicked the ball
Bullseye; she were out cold on the ground

I tell you there weren't half a rumpus
Crowd were starting to scoff
They shouted 'Put her up front for Stanley'
As they stretchered poor Doris off

They carried her to St. John ambulance room
I followed on behind
And as I opened door to hut
I should have guessed just what I'd find

Her in a St John uniform
And in attendance Bert and Len
She were holding a sponge to Doris's head
I said. 'So you two are at it again'

'They only popped in to say hello
You think I'm interested in Bert and Len?
When I might be called away any minute
To lay healing hands on twenty two fit men'

CHARITIES AND CHURCH FETES

Lifeguards and Shirring Elastic
Short Shorts and Plimsolls
Pink Shorts and Wellies
Gypsies and White Elephants

LIFEGUARDS AND SHIRRING ELASTIC

'Doris' I said. 'What were you thinking of
Volunteering us for this?
I can't honestly say we can do it
I think we should give it a miss'

She said. 'Elsie, it'll do us good
Lack of exercise is a sin
Dig out your old cozzie and swimming cap
We're going to *do* this sponsored swim'

'I'm not going to buy a new costume
I've had one since I were a girl'
I said. 'Doris, shirring elastic isn't in vogue
But never mind, you give it a whirl'

I asked. 'Bert, are you doing it with us?
It'll be good for you and Len
Apart from lifting t' remote control
You get no exercise you men'

'I don't think we'll bother, but you go ahead
We've a bit of business on'
I said. 'No doubt you're going to bookies
Then calling round at hers, over yon'

We arrived at pool at th'appointed time
We stuffed our shoes and frocks in t'lockers
Doris stood there in her old bathing suit
I said. 'Eee it doesn't do much for your
……..figure'

'Eh up, they all look young 'uns
Well us two, won't stand a chance
They'll clock 60 or 70 lengths at a time
And lead us a merry old dance'

We climbed down steps at shallow end
Starter shouter. 'Right ladies off you go
I want twenty lengths from both of you
We've to raise some money you know'

We managed one, we managed two
Then Doris started to sink
Lifeguard jumped in and holding her up
Gave the starter an almighty wink

Her cozzie top had come adrift
Shirring elastic had let her down
Then the local reporter's camera flashed
She said. 'Oh no! I'll be all over town'

'Someone throw a lifebelt
They're obviously starting to tire
No just a minute she's got one'
I said. 'No, that's Doris's spare tyre'

Well they got her to the poolside
I said. 'Quick, give her the kiss of life'
'Well I'm not doing it' the lifeguard said
'Where's her husband, she's *his* wife?'

Thank goodness she had no ill effects
Though she'd swallowed a pint or two
And by the time we'd had a pot of tea
We'd come round a bit us two

I said. 'Well we won't have raised
much money
But we got plenty of funny looks
So Derian House'll just have to wait
'Til we sell a few more books'

SHORT SHORTS AND PLIMSOLLS

I said. 'I think we'll do this Race for Life
Down at Witton Park
We could raise some cash for charity
And besides it'll be a lark'

'I'm not so sure,' said Doris
'I haven't run for years'
I said. 'We'll jog round block a time or two
That'll help to calm our fears'

Bert said, 'Me and Len'll train you
We have done it before'
'But only whippets,' Len replied
'But these two, I'm not so sure'

'Well we're going to do it, Doris,' I said
'Never mind what them two say
Me and you'll be up with the leaders
On Wednesday June 23rd, race day'

So we found our holiday t-shirts
Two pairs of old school pumps
We bought some shorts down charity shop
But they didn't half show our lumps

Monday evening we both set off
At a fair jog down our street
She's stood in doorway at number four
'Looks like men are in for a treat'

'Take no notice of her, ' I said
'Well I hope you're not going to run far?
Talk about a couple of movers
I reckon you need a sports bra'

Them two were stood on the corner
Stopwatch in their hand
Bert in his old Addidas
And Len with this lurid sweatband

'Come on girls, keep going
Round corner and up next street
You're doing well,' Bert shouted
'Elsie pick up your feet'

We ran 'til we were exhausted
And both that red in the face
W e came up against what's known as
the 'The Wall'
'Cos we were weaving all over the place

We came to a halt outside chip shop
Puffed out, we started to wheeze
Guess who were sat in the window
Eating fish, chips and mushy peas?

Her hand on Leonard's stopwatch
And poor Doris all out of sorts
She were sat there in this little crop top
And them legs in the shortest of shorts

'We're only talking tactics,' Len said
'On how to win the race
She reckons she could bribe the judge
To give you two a place'

'And you're training her for that?' I puffed
As I tipped peas on her head
'If I were you, I'd get home quick
Before you're left for dead'

But both of us are determined
We're going to do that race
Bert and Len can carry our handbags
And *she'd* better not show her face

So come June twenty third
We'll be on that starting line
And we just might surprise her
And run it in right a good time

PINK SHORTS AND WELLIES

It didn't half rain I can tell you
Last night at Witton Park
We'd been training for The Race for Life
We hoped to get round before dark

Len and Bert were there to support us
Said they'd follow as close as they could
'But I'd put your wellies on,' Bert said
'There's an awful lot of mud'

Doris fell, as we'd just set off
Me and this woman give her a hoist
She hitched up her soggy pants and said
'It's been years since I felt this moist'

Then we spotted this slapper in full make up
I said. 'Well it looks like her from the back
Bright pink shorts, false tan on legs
Blonde hair, like a haystack'

She waved and came across to us
She said, 'Well now I've seen the dregs
Running in wellies you won't get far
I said, 'Rain has streaked your legs'

We started off with aerobics
Suppose to warm us up
We didn't bother we'd got the flask
Rum and coffee, we both had a cup

Half past seven we started to jog
She were right it's not easy in wellies
We spotted Leanne on the BBC bus
But we were hoping to get on the tele

That hill's a bit of a killer
But Bert and Len they cheered us on
We clung to each other and reached the top
Hoping we'd nearly done

One K, two K still going strong
We'd lost sight of Bert and Len
'Don't worry,' I said. 'They won't be far
It won't be long before we spot 'em again'

Pink shorts were bobbin' up ahead
Like two ferrets in a bag
Doris were puffing and wheezing
We were both beginning to lag

Three K, four K and still it rained
I said. 'Come on we've got to go on'
Pink shorts seemed to be missing
I said. 'Eh up! Number 4, she's gone'

'She'll have given up' said Doris,
'Stamina's not her thing'
'Well not for running' I replied
'But she's stamina for being a plaything'

On we jogged down this narrow path
In bushes, a flash of pink
We came to a halt, I said, 'Over there
Doris, what do you think?'

Them two in attendance
Massaging them streaky brown pins
'Just what are you doing?' I bellowed
'Just trying to make sure she wins'

'Well then your a couple of losers'
I must say they both looked troubled
'You can leave *her* here we're going home
And you're sponsor money? well it's just
doubled'

GYPSYS AND WHITE ELEPHANTS

Elsie said. 'Do you fancy going
down t'village?
They're holding a garden fete
I reckon we should go down there
It'd be a change at any rate'

There were a cake stall and Tombola
And a gypsy in a tent
Plant stalls and white elephant
We were really glad we went

We bought chocolate cakes and ivy
Then decided we'd have a fling
We got four tickets for Tombola
But we didn't win a thing

I said. 'I reckon we should have us palms read
'Cos this last year hasn't been good'
Mind you when we got there
We wondered if we should

I poked my head through a slit in t'tent
It were all dark and kind of smelly
Beaded curtains, a dim red lamp
Just like that one at our Nellie's

'Come in,' she said. 'Now don't be shy
You look a couple of sad cases
You've had your share of troubles
I can see it in your faces'

'How's she know,' I said. 'Elsie
I reckon we should risk a pound
And who knows she might tell us summat
Her judgment could be sound'

She were sat behind this table
Her scent mysterious and heady
Her face in shadow, scarf pulled down
Crystal ball at the ready

'Cross my palm with silver
Ask me what you want to know'
'So long as it's two for the price of one'
I said, just to let her know'

'Well you see we've been having a
bit of bother
With other women and the like
Our husbands are unfaithful and lazy
It fact I think they must be on strike'

'I can see your husbands aren't happy
I see two discontented men
They're wondering should they call it quits
They wouldn't marry again'

'One of em's coming into money
I can see him traveling far
I see a rusty three-wheeler
Oh! He's driving a brand new car'

'I reckon nowt to this,' I said
'Is there nothing good for us?'
'Well you are ladies of a certain age
You can go half price on t'bus'

'I've had enough,' said Elsie
And she knocked crystal ball to the floor
As the gypsy stood up, her scarf slipped
It were her from number four

'I were only doing vicar a favour
I were OK 'til along came you two
Anyroad do you like my gypsy outfit?
And by the way most of it's true'

'It just isn't fair, I said 'Elsie
We never win at all'
'Never mind,' she said. 'Nothing changes
Let's see what's on white elephant stall'

'Have you got any bargains left?
Summat that might do for our men'
'Well I had two nearly new flat caps
But gypsy bought 'em for Bert and Len'

HOLIDAYS AND HIGH DAYS

Hot Cross Buns and Bruises
Bank Holiday Ton
Boarding Houses and Lost Dentures
Two Lips from Amsterdam
French Francs and Frogs Legs

HOT CROSS BUNS AND BRUISES

Easter can be a lovely time
Or not, as the case might be
Last year it were pretty disastrous
But then things are for Doris and me

Good Friday we've this tradition
We walk over Whalley Nab
Len and Bert don't get much exercise
We *need* to get rid of the flab

So we set off nice and early
I were just locking my front door
'Where you all off to?' she shouted
Her from number four

'It's none of your business,' said Doris
'And no, you're not coming with us
We're going in our Len's three-wheeler
You want to go out, go on t'bus'

We all clambered into Reliant
Tied rucksack wi' butties on top
Then Bert said. 'Hang on a minute
There's something I've forgot'

We sat there patiently waiting
'Oh where has he gone to now?'
In rear view mirror, he were talking to her
I said. 'There's gonna be a row'

He got back in and off we set
I said, 'I suppose you were talking
about nowt?'
He said. 'We were only passing the time of day
And she were saying, she weren't going out'

We parked Reliant up when we got to the Nab
River sparkled in the sun
Len said. 'I hate this walk Good Friday
I don't know why we come'

'Because we're not leaving you at home
You two, we just don't trust
And besides that it'll do you good
Your joints are starting to rust'

Well we'd walked about a mile or two
We were well into our hike
A bicycle bell, a flash of pink
It were her on a mountain bike

She winked as she passed and gave a shout
'I'll see you t'other side o't'hill'
And as she said it she hit a stone
She didn't half take a spill

'She's out cold,' said Len. 'what do we do?'
And he looked at Doris and me
'With shorts like them she will be cold'
I said. 'Get her to th'A and E'

They picked her up as best they could
And she made this moaning noise
I said. 'Right you two, it's two miles back
This'll sort out men from boys'

'Doris, me and you might as well sit down
We'll have our sandwiches here
Then we'll walk down to village and
call in the pub
And we'll have a nice cold beer'

It were near tea time when we got there
I tell you we could have cried
Them two and her in pub window
Reliant parked outside

Pink shorts hardly covering them legs
I said. 'You two can't resist floozies
And *you* came round pretty sharpish
And you can stop rubbing her bruises'

So this Easter we've decided we're
going to stop in
Them two can paint backyard shed
Me and Doris can eat hot cross buns
And Easter eggs instead

BANK HOLIDAY TON

I said, 'Doris let's go to Morecambe
It's always been our favourite haunt
We're not stoppin' in this Bank Holiday
Let's go out on a jaunt'

She said. 'We'll take the scenic route,
through Trough
And get us some fresh air
Pack some butties, but leave the flask
We'll have nettle beer when we get there'

So we set off in Robin Reliant
It's grand, now she's' passed her test
We left Bert and Len front o'telly
They said they needed the rest

We'd been driving about an hour or so
When Reliant started to splutter
'Something's sadly wrong I think'
Said Doris, all of a flutter

We got out and stood by side o' road
I said. 'Aren't you a member of th' AA
And lifting bonnet and peering in, she said
'We were, but Len wouldn't pay'

I walked round car, kicked all three wheels
Just as a gang of bikers roared past
'I don't like the look of them,' Doris said
'I'm glad they've gone flying past'

'Eh up,' I said. 'They're coming back
Quick get back in the car'
We tried in vain to start it up
We weren't going to get very far

This enormous fella approached us
He looked like Meatloaf on speed
Skull and Crossbones on t'jacket
Chains hanging down to his knees

'Are you two old dolls in trouble then?'
I said, 'Doris is he talking to us?'
She said primly. 'No thanks we can manage
Unless you've a timetable for bus'

'Well this old heap's about had it'
I heard Doris give a sigh
'Right hop on back, we'll escort you home
Come on now, don't be shy'

He lifted Doris on pillion with ease
I could tell she'd got in a strop
With her handbag, her brolly,
then this helmet on
And she tied her rain mate on top

I climbed on back of another myself
He shouted. 'Right Mrs. hold on tight
We'll get you home in double quick time
We can do a ton all right'

We'd gone five miles before I opened my eyes
I could see Doris at the front of the pack
I thought, I don't believe it,: I'm enjoying this
I don't want them to hurry back

In no time we were back in Clitheroe
Reality, with a jolt
Brolly came open like a parachute
As we came roaring to a halt

Front door opened, them two came out
And stood with mouths open wide
'Where's Robin Reliant gone?' asked Len
I said. 'Well bloomin' thing sorta died'

'And you can take your hands off that man,'
said Bert
'What do you think you're doing with this lot?'
'Getting up to speed and enjoying ourselves
We've joined Hells Angels, that's what'

BOARDING HOUSES AND LOST DENTURES

You can't beat a day or two in Blackpool
We felt we needed a break
Them two botherin' with her across road
Has caused us a lot of heart ache

We booked in a smashin' boarding house
Bed, breakfast and evening meal
It's called Del Casa Rosa
Mind you roses round door aren't real

You know Doris came here on her honeymoon
Unfortunately she had to bring Len
Said it hadn't been a pleasant experience
They'd not be holidaying in same room again

Me and her have got a lovely room
Bathroom just across t'hall
We haven't half got a nice sea view
Theirs looks over backyard wall

Morning, we left them two in bed
And went down on the sand
We tucked our skirts in our knickers
And paddled in sea, hand in hand

Doris said. 'I fancy a donkey ride'
But poor beast got in a state
As she climbed on the saddle slipped
And it's knees buckled with the weight

We'd arranged to meet at Harry Ramsden's
When it were time to have some dinner
Bert said. 'We're going down bookies
this afternoon
We're hoping to back a winner'

I said. 'Come on we'll go to Pleasure Beach
We can catch the tram down there'
Then we spotted the Big One
She said. 'Elsie which one of us dares?'

'We'll go together,' I said bravely
But at top it were a long way beneath
Me hat flew off as we came flying down
But poor Doris lost her top teeth

I can tell you we were all of a quiver
I said. 'We'll never do that again'
'And whash can I do abouth me top shet'
Lisped Doris, face screwed up in pain

'Well you can go to dentist tomorrow' I said
'Stop fussing you look alright
Just put a bit of extra lippy on
We've to meet them two in Tower tonight'

Course we couldn't spot 'em when
we got there
But by heck we got a surprise
When lights went out and this man appeared
And his big organ began to rise

We'd a couple of valletta's, then we
went back home
Landlady said. 'Police have been round tonight
Your husbands were drunk and disorderly
So they've locked 'em in cells overnight'

Next morning we went down to station
Oh my goodness the state of them two
'I wonder if they might keep 'em' I said
Wishful thinking as you do

But no, they let 'em out with a caution
Doris asked.'Can you bribe the poleesh'
'No madame you can't, and if I were you
I'd spend me money getting new teeth'

TWO LIPS FROM AMSTERDAM

'Doris' I said. 'What a nice surprise
Them two booking a three-day break
They won't say where we're going
It's a surprise for heavens sake'

Come Friday we were up at the crack of dawn
We'd a fair rush to catch the bus
Three cases, two hold alls and a trolley
Seemed a lot for us

Off we went down the motorway
Plenty of stops for cuppas and t' loo
It's a slow job getting folk on and off
We always seem to wait for *them* two

We were surprised when we got on a ferry
I said, 'I bet it's romantic Paree'
But Bert winked at Len and tapped his nose
'You'll just have to wait and see'

Well crossing got a bit stormy
It were good to be back on dry land
Leonard were struggling to walk straight
We'd all to give him a hand

We got back on bus and all fell asleep
Then just as sun were beginning to going down
Bert woke us up by shouting
'We're just about going to hit town'

There were a hek of a lot of traffic
Red lights all over the place
I said. 'Doris them two are enjoying themselves
Look at the smile on their face'

It were late when we got to our lodgings
It were all we could do to unpack
I said, 'Doris we'll see you tomorrow
It's time we all hit the sack'

When we looked out'a window next morning
All we could see were bridges and bikes
'Doris' I said. 'We're in old Amsterdam
Isn't it here where you get lots of dykes?'

'Right first time', said Leonard
'You've always wanted to come here
We've arranged a trip for you 'round bulb fields
So here's some Euros my dears'

Heaven knows where them two were going
But they bought some detailed street maps
On way back to t'hotel we went shopping
We bought clogs and a couple of Dutch Caps

We'd arranged to meet at three for a coffee
I said. 'I reckon they're going to give it a miss'
Then we spotted 'em coming out of this house
And girl in window blew 'em a kiss

'And where have you two been?' I asked
'You both look hot and flustered'
'Just having a bit of culture and a stroll',
Bert said
'And window shopping'. Leonard blustered

Going back on bus the following day
I said. 'We should give them two what for
And I bet they've brought summat
back with them
To give to her at number four'

Just what have they been buying
I bet it's summat flimsy and red
Whatever it is I can be sure
We wouldn't wear it to bed

We saw 'em nip across when
we got back home
She stood in t'doorway tryin' to look glam
I said. 'I bet I know what they
brought her back
It'll be two lips from Old Amsterdam'

But no they gave her a brown parcel
But before they got to front door
A tarty red basque with suspenders fell out
And landed in a heap on the floor

Well they've just about blown it this time
We'll not be going again
And if we do decide to go away
We'll be going without our men.

FRENCH FRANCS AND FROGS LEGS

Here we are in Dover
Sitting on a train
'Oh Doris' I said. 'What we doing?
I'll not do this again'

Bert, Len and me and Doris
I reckon we're all taking a chance
On this outing with the Monday Club
To a Hypermarket in France

'If there's on thing I hate it's a tunnel
Oh why did we book on this trip
And what are them two whisperin' about
I wish we were going on t'ship'

'Well it's too late now' said Doris
'We seem to be on our way
Shut your eyes 'till we come up on t'other side
It's not going to take us all day'

'I'm not closing my eyes' said Doris
'I hope we won't go too fast
You know I don't like to miss things
We might spot some fish swimming past'

Bert and Len were sat three seats down
And I were just going to give 'em a shout
To say I'd unpacked the croissants
When all bloomin' lights went out

Talk about pandemonium
I said 'Doris I'm having a fit'
She said. 'At least we're together in same boat'
I said. 'Don't you mean under it'

Lights flickered twice and came back on
Then again we were on our way
'Oo la la, here we go' said Bert
I said. 'Don't you go getting risque'

Chara were waiting when we came out
To take us to the superstore
Bert and Len were grinning ear to ear
What had we brought them for?

It were massive when we got there
Aisles plenty wide enough
Beer and wine, champagne and cheese
Some very fancy stuff

'I think we'll split up' I said to Bert
'We're better off going our own way
You go and get your beer and fags
We can all meet up when we pay'

We bought l'escargot, cheese and garlic
And frogs legs in a tin
They were already at checkout wi'trolley
So we piled our purchases in

'Vous cannot pay with these m'seur'
I shouted. 'Where did you get them francs?'
'This fella gave me a good deal for my euros
Outside, stood by taxi rank'

'What do you want to do Madame?'
.'Well it's all piled up now in basket
Oh, pass us me handbag Doris' I said
'I'll have to give her me plastic'

'So that's another disastrous trip
I'll just have to get a loan'
'And we've that horrible tunnel to face
Before we get these two home'

Well Frog's legs turned out to be slimy
And garlic, phew! what a stench
Bert's in parlour reciting 'Je suis Bert'
They've decided they're going to learn French

IT NEVER RAINS BUT IT POURS

Raindrops and Mobile Phones
Raindrops and Ice Creams

RAINDROPS AND MOBILE PHONES

You'd never believe last Friday
Talk about soaking wet ground
There were a cloud burst over Whalley
Me and Doris nearly drowned

It all started at five thirty
As we left work for home
We'd gone in Len's Robin Reliant
Good job we'd his mobile phone

We'd parked 'cross road up a back passage
We try avoiding yellow lines
Bert and Len are always moaning
Fed up of paying the fines

Lollipop man stood at the crossing
Waders right up to his crutch
He were carrying women to t'other side
But didn't like look of us much

He said. 'By gum you two are big 'uns
I've got me work cut out here
I'll tackle her with glasses first
But I'm not carrying t'other, no fear'

Well he picked me up in a fireman's lift
Poor chap could hardly stand
I said.'Don't bother we'll tuck our skirts up
And paddle across hand in hand'

Luckily we'd parked on a piece of high ground
We'd no problem opening the door
But we'd only gone a hundred yards
When water came seeping through floor

The boys in blue were on duty
Knee deep in water, waving cars through
He put his hand up to stop us
But we floated straight past, as you do

I said.'Doris do you remember that James Bond
film
When Astin Martin turned into a boat?'
And as we floated past Maureen Cookson's
window
She said.'Eee that's a nice dress and coat'

We came to a halt in the car park
To be honest it were more like a lake
I said 'Doris, moor us up to that lamppost
I've had just as much as I can take'

'There's that mobile in me handbag
We'd better call Bert and Len
We need 'em here pretty sharpish
Before we float off again'

'How do I do it?' said Doris
'Well Len said just press number one
Nothing seems to be happening
I think receptions gone'

'Let's try something different
Why don't you lean out'a door
Oh, wait a minute it's ringing
'Hello it's Samantha from number 4'

'Well I think we'd better abandon ship
And take our chances in t'flood
If we'd managed to get hold of them two
It wouldn't have done any good'

Well we squelched home at half past seven
Like drowned rats Doris and me
Them two's sat watching football
Shouted 'What we having for tea?'

'After all difficulties we've been through
Your lucky to see Doris and me
Try pressing number one on t'mobile
And go over there for your tea'

RAINDROPS AND ICE CREAMS

We'd booked a day or two in Fleetwood
Lovely B and B
Pity Bert and Len had come
But they like it by the sea

Weather weren't right brilliant
Just our luck again
In morning we played pitch and put
Not much fun in rain

We had fish and chips for t'dinner
Fleetwood's famous for it's fish
I said. 'Let's lose them two for th'afternoon
Then us two can do as we wish'

They didn't mind us going
Said they'd go back to digs for a sleep
'They'll be up to no good,' I said, 'Doris
Men! I tell you they make you weep'

We wandered down to market
I said. 'Right let's have some fun'
But it started raining hard again
Then we spotted this Mystery Run

'It's a fiver a piece,' said driver
'Hop on girls, for trip of your life
You could end up almost anywhere with me
And you can see I haven't brought wife'

'He's a bit of a card,' said Doris
'Quite a gleam, in his eye
Fancy calling us two girls'
I said. 'He's taking our money, that's why'

Before long we were out in the country
But trees they were all dripping wet
I said. 'These roads look familiar
It'll be Ribble Valley, I bet'

'A fiver each to come back home'
Driver said. 'Right folks, I'll just park it
Then you can have a good look round
It's famous is Clitheroe Market'

We went in Swales' and had some tea
I said. 'This'll do for us
Then we'll have a look round Dawson's
Before we get back on the bus'

'Next stop Ossie Mills' he said
'But on way there's this beauty spot
It's called Spring Wood near Whalley
And I reckon you'll like it a lot'

'It's pouring rain,' I said, 'Doris'
'Cheer up,' she said, 'it'll be fine
There's a kiosk by the entrance
I'll buy us a ninety nine'

Chara pulled up on car park
I said. 'Doris, I'm sure that's your car
Next to kiosk, that Reliant
What on earth is that there for?'

'We'd better investigate,' she said
'Things might not be what they seem'
But sat there in back o' kiosk
Them two, eating ice cream

They weren't right pleased to see us
I said. 'What have you two come here for?'
And hidden behind 'em wi' ice cream scoop
Were her from number four

'Have you seen what your Len's wearing
Where's he got that pink plastic mac?'
'He's only trying it on for a bit of fun,'
'Well he'd better give it you back'

'Right, you can run us home quick, sharpish'
I said, rain dripping from my hat
'Then back to Fleetwood for luggage, you two
And that's the end of that'

NOTABLE DATES

A Penny for Doris
Warts and All
Valentines and Dirty Washing

A PENNY FOR DORIS

Well I'll tell you what, me and Doris
We're not doing it again, no fear
We'll not be having a bonfire
Not after what happened last year

We'd been collecting wood for ages
Piling it up in our backyard
Getting a commode and a three piece suite
Through back gate, well, it's quite hard

Morning o'bonfire we went to get fireworks
Bert and Len were making the guy
'We're not showing you,' said Leonard
'We want it to be a surprise'

In th'afternoon they built up the bonfire
While we cooked up a treat
Toffee apples, parkin and black-eyed peas
Enough to feed all t'street

Come evening we were all excited
'Cos we're all big kids at heart
I said, 'Doris, where's our Bert and Len?
It's time for festivities to start'

Well fireworks were spectacular
And flames were leaping high
I said, 'Right, when bonfire dies down a bit
Them two can bring out the guy'

They carried it out between 'em
On an old chair made out of wood
All street started laughing and clapping
'Oh, it just *like* her – *isn't* it good!!'

And there she were, in all her splendour
It weren't fair of them, to mock
It were spittin' image of Doris
Right down to grey wig and best frock

I saw her face start to crumple
Then she started to shout at her Len
'I know you two haven't made that by yourself
You've bin across road again'

'W-w-well we needed help,'
stammered Leonard
'We couldn't begin to try
And she said it would be a talking point
To have a female guy'

'So you thought it were a good idea
Well then you two can take the blame
Winning lottery ticket in that frock pocket
And now it's *gone* up in flames'

So we've had a bit of business,
this November 5th
Though we said we wouldn't bother at all
But there's a guy with high heels; 38 double D
Propped up against number four's wall

WARTS AND ALL

If you watch the sky on Halloween
When the moon is riding high
And the wind is moaning in the trees
You might see two witches pedaling by

We were on Bert and Leonard's tandem
Our legs could only just reach
And to make it look more authentic
We carried a broomstick apiece

We'd hired two witches' costumes
And borrowed next doors cat
Didn't need stick on warts, 'cos we've got 'em
And we both wore a pointed hat

'Doris,' I said. 'We need a swede
To hollow out and insert a candle'
She said. 'Don't you think those foreign men
Are a bit too hot to handle'

I said. 'No,Doris you've got it wrong
I didn't mean a fella
What we need is a bit of light
Oh go and get a torch from t' cellar'

You see we live in the shadow of Pendle
That awe-inspiring hill
So we decided to go and cast a few spells
As we'd a couple of hours to kill

We thought we'd go trick or treating
We know just what to do
In the past we've tricked many a man
And treated one or two

We pedaled to the top of the village
Whalley had never seen such a sight
Witches weeds flying behind us
Onwards into the night

We flew so fast, we lost our hats
The cat could hardly keep pace
'Doris' I said. 'I'm enjoying this
It feels like we're in the Milk Race'

We knocked on the first house we came to
The door flew open wide
Constable Jones were standing there
He said, 'You two get inside'

'This phone it hasn't stopped ringing
Just what have you got to say?
Pedaling round disturbing the peace
Someone's phoned RSPCA'

'Hubble Bubble Toil and Trouble
We didn't mean any harm sir
We were only trick or treating
And cat's only lost some fur'

'Take off that wart and silly hat
Next time there'll be a fine'
'Hat can come off,' said Doris
'But I'm afraid the wart is mine'

So if you're out and about on Halloween
And you look up into the sky
Don't blink twice, or you'll miss us
Doris and Elsie pedaling by

VALENTINES AND DIRTY WASHING

So there we both were Valentines Day
Sat in Launder-ette
Watching mucky washing spin round
How romantic can you get?

Fella sat next to us has fallen asleep
Daily Sport on his head
'Well at least some fellas come here
Unlike our two' Doris said

'Bert said he had sent me a card, I said
When I took him up his toast
He couldn't understand why it hadn't arrived
Said it must have got lost in the post'

'Well mine hasn't come either,' said Doris
'We get nothing from our men
I bought Len socks with hearts on last year
But I've never seen 'em again'

'And speaking of hearts and Valentines
I bet *she'll* be coming in?
Washing her dirty linen in public
And we all know where it's bin'

'Are there any driers free?'
'Ey up, here she comes,' I said
'I've washed these in me new machine
They're sheets from me water bed'

Course she managed to show her stocking tops
When she bent down to shove clothes in drier
Bedding and her frillies all bundled in
And her skirt couldn't get much higher

Then this fella sat next to us came to life
It's amazing how men re-act
To a slapper like her and a bit of thigh
The amount of trouble *she* can attract!

'I don't think they'll all fit in,' she said
He asked 'Do you want me to re-arrange?'
It takes 20 pees, not pound coins
But don't worry, I've plenty of small change'

We sat there watching her clothes tumble dry
Summat black flashed past now and then
I said, 'look Doris black socks with hearts on
Aren't *they* what you bought for your Len?'

'I can't believe my eyes,' cried Doris
I think I'm going to have a bit of a do'
'Well I'd hang on,' I said 'Have a proper one
Matching underpants have just come in view'

TWO LIFE SENTENCES

Gondolas and Creaky Corsets
Anniversaries and Glowing Faces

GONDOLAS AND CREAKY CORSETS

I called round to see Doris, day after
She'd been on this trip for a day
Her and Len had been to Venice
She'd come home in a right bad way

They'd got to th'airport at crack 'o dawn
It were going to be romantic you see
Just her and Leonard were going
For their Ruby Aniversar-ee

They'd had to go through security
And *she* hadn't half med a din
This woman said she'd have to frisk her
But she pointed at this fella. 'I'll have him'

'Well you can't have' the woman said
Put your bag on th' X Ray'
So she told her if she found owt she
could keep it
She'd nothing to hide, no way

Course Len said, 'We'd have wings, were we
meant to fly
You can't beat your own two feet'
'Shut up and take of your cap,' Doris had said
'And sit yourself down in your seat'

Then he mentioned joining this exclusive club
Said it were called, 'The Mile High'
'Well you'll not be joining with me,' she'd said
'There'll be no funny business up in the sky'

Well they'd been up in th'air an hour or so
Then she wanted to go to loo
She squeezed past Len and walked up the aisle
To the back of the plane like you do

On her return she couldn't see him
He weren't in same seat as before
Then she spotted him sat right down at the front
With a redhead in row number four

He said he were pointing out landmarks
If she looked French Alps were beneath
So Doris told her. 'He's bald beneath that cap
And them's certainly not his own teeth'

When they'd finally got to Venice
It had taken her by surprise
She'd gazed round in awe and wonder
She couldn't believe her eyes

She'd said shops were lovely but ever so dear
Café's didn't know what to ask
And they didn't seem to like 'em sitting there
With their own butties and a flask

She'd booked this gondola for half past two
Bert said he'd sit in St Marks Square
This brawny man in a striped T- Shirt
Sized her up when she got herself there

He'd spoken in rapid Italian
And stretched his arms out wide
'He seemed to be weighing me up,' she said
Then she decided he were talking about tide

He'd taken her on a wonderful trip
All round canals more or less
She were disappointed he hadn't sung a note
But he did seem a bit out of breath

He were bright red in the face when
he got her back
And as she thanked him for the ride
It happened – she'd one leg left in the boat
When it floated away from the side

She said it had fairly made her corsets creak
Now she's a problem when she sits
And it'll be a while before she goes again
To Venice, to do the splits

ANNIVERSARIES AND GLOWING FACES

It were Elsie and Bert's anniversary
It had been a long hard trail
Marriage, it's like hard labour
Two life sentences in jail

Can you believe it, 40 years?
Goodness knows how she's managed to stay
I've had plenty of bother with my Len
But not like her; no way

Now when it were our Ruby Wedding
Me and Len went to Venice for day
But I said. 'Elsie if *you* want a bit of a do
You can have it at our house, OK?'

It took me a week to plan it
I had to cater for ten
With me and Len and eight on her side
I don't think I'd do it again

We had fish and beef paste butties
Cheese and pineapple on sticks
But by time I'd made the trifle
I were beginning to feel quite sick

I sent Len down to th'Off License
But he came back with nowt but beer
'Champagne's over a fiver a bottle,' he said
'I'm not paying that much, no fear'

'Well we'll just have to mek a do' I said
But I have planned another surprise
I've ordered Elsie a kiss-a-gram
She'll never believe her eyes'

'It's a fella dressed up as Tarzan
Toned pecs, bronzed body on show
And *I'll* be having a good gander,'I said
Just to let him know

Well they all turned up at eight o'clock
By then I were red in the face
Then they sang 'For he's a jolly good fellow'
Which did seem a bit out of place

But Elsie didn't seem to mind
Standing there in her best frock
She got tiddly and made this little speech
About how her Bert were her rock

About half past nine the doorbell rang
I thought, It's him, as I dashed to the door
Stood there in basque and suspenders
Were her from number four

'I've ordered Elsie a Tarzan,' I said
I must say I sounded curt
'Well he's on his way, he won't be long
I've come as a freebie for Bert'

She pushed straight past me,
grabbed hold of Bert
And sat down on his knee
All fellas started clapping and shouting
Elsie shook her head at me

'I'm going home' she said sadly
Tears coming to her eyes
And as she walked down garden path,
There stood Tarzan, *what* a size!!

Picked her up in a fireman's lift
He managed it all right
And we didn't see either of them again
For rest o' party night

Following morning I popped next door
She said' I'm sorry I had to go'
She looked like she needed a good nights sleep
But her face had a lovely glow.

'Bert's fast asleep in bed' she said
'I must say he seems quite jealous'
'So it all turned out for the best?' I asked
And she answered, 'It sure as Hell as'

ONE WEDDING AND A FUNERAL

All Creatures Great and Small
Legacy and Toupeés

ALL CREATURES GREAT AND SMALL

We enjoy a good wedding, Doris and me
We nearly always shed a tear
But Bert and Len didn't want to go to this one
Because they were both riddled with fear

You see this time it were a funny occasion
It were hers from number four
Dressed all in virginal white again
Though she's done it three times before

I said. 'Them two'll be quaking in their shoes
When vicar asks, does anyone
know just cause?
I can think of a few times she 's led
them two astray
And how many more- heaven knows'

Of course me and Doris were turned out a treat
But we didn't want to sit with them two
There were a funny smell coming from
Len's trousers
So we sat behind 'em in't next pew

You see Len had his ferret in his pocket
It made no difference how poor Doris cursed
He said. 'I'm not leaving her at home
on her own
First litter's due and it's always the worst'

So there we were all listening to th'organ
As she comes teetering down the aisle
Pity the poor fella she's trapped this time
Her antics'll soon wipe of *his* silly smile

All things Bright and Beautiful,
Fight the Good Fight
Love Divine and O Happy Day
'Funny selection of hymns,' Doris, said
'Then coming out to I Did it My Way'

Her sister Lilly brought up the rear
Manfully carrying her train
I said. 'Doris, she's just caught your Len's eye
And she's winked at him again'

We all stood outside in't pouring rain
Photographer took a photo or two
They were a double decker bus on stand by
To take us to Coop for the do

Meal turned out quite a good one
Sherry trifle and a nice ham tea
Bert and Len drank best bitter
Asti Spumanti for Doris and me

As the evening wore on they got drunker
I said. 'Doris can you see what I see?
That floozie's sister Lilly
Has plonked herself down on Len's knee'

She cooed. 'I don't half like a nice big man'
Then tickling him under chin, she giggled
She looked down at his lap,
then leapt up in alarm
Screaming. 'Something bit me and then
sort of wriggled'

'That'll teach you,' I said. 'To leave men alone
Playing fast and loose has no merit'
'Lilly, if you want him,
you can have him,' said Doris
'But he comes with a family of ferrets'

'She's as bad as her sister, Doris,' I said
As we waved t'happy couple goodbye
'And it won't be her last wedding
we come too'
Added Doris, with a sigh

Anyroad we went back to our house
and took of our shoes
I made us a nice pot of tea
And Bert and Len and the ferrets?
Well they were all fast asleep on settee

LEGACYS AND TOUPEÉS

Well we've had a bit of an upset
Len's Uncle Fred has passed away
I said to Doris. 'I reckon you'll be alright
He'll have put a bit away'

She said, 'Well he never got married
Said he didn't need a wife
Didn't go on many holidays
Worked hard all of his life'

'So you could be in for a couple o' bob
You and Len just might let lucky
You know saying where there's dirt
there's money
And *his* windows were certainly mucky'

On day of funeral we all sat in church
Surprising, they were quite a few
'Doris,' I said. 'Look whose over there
All in black, sat in front pew'

'She looks like a black widow spider
What *she's* doing here, heaven knows
Veil over her face and that silly black hat
Clutching a single red rose'

'I didn't know she knew our Fred'
I said. 'Doris, she's had a few men
What makes you think she were exclusive
To my Bert and your Len'

'Well nothing surprises me any more
Eh up, here comes the vicar
Anyroad we'll have to wait 'til will is read
To see if you've got any nicker'

Prayers were said and t'hymns were sung
Then as Uncle Fred came up th'aisle
The floozie placed her rose on the coffin
And gave me and Doris a big smile

Refreshments afterward were served at Co-op
We'd a nice bit of ham for our tea
'Course *she* managed to eat three trifles
There were none left for Doris and me

She drank to much sherry and got tipsy
Her hat it were all askew
Then Bert and Len rushed to her aid
Ever gentlemen, them two

So here we all are in solicitors
Waiting for will to be read
'Unusual bequests Mr and Mrs Rawbottom
It might be as well your Fred's dead'

He intoned, 'I Fred Rawbottom being
of sound mind
To my nephew Len I bequeath
Me toupeé, as he's going thin on top
And to his wife, me new set of teeth'

'And all me money, me house and me bike
And everything in me top drawer
For services happily rendered
I leave to my girlfriend at no 4'

'Right,' I said. 'Doris here's the plan
We're going to have to take this tack
Let's encourage 'em both to keep going round
Then we might plough a few quid back'

THE NHS

Hot Flushes and Red Cheeks
Loose Teeth and Women

HOT FLUSHES AND RED CHEEKS

Me and Doris have been having problems
Hot flushes and the like
Experiencing terrible mood swings
Waking up at night

Tossing and turning all through night
And they like their sleep, do Bert and Len
'It's time you got some sleeping pills'
Bert said. 'I were awake all night, again'

So me and Doris made an appointment
I said. 'Doctor won't mind if we share'
There we were, sat in waiting room
She said, 'have you seen whose over there?'

Smirking over her magazine
That trollop from number four
'I've decided to go back on pill' she said
'What have you two come here for?'

'Ignore her' I said. 'Pill indeed
She's all of forty five'
'Well she seems to do summat for our two'
Said Doris, 'with us two they're barely alive'

Anyroad we went in to see the doctor
He were lovely with Doris and me
He listened sympathetically
Then sent us out with HRT

Well we got these patches from chemist
Like see through elastoplast
Stuck 'em on where it didn't show
An a week later what a contrast

We were managing to get a good nights rest
No need for hot milk and whisky
Thank goodness they weren't doing
what we'd feared
We didn't want to feel frisky

And Bert were sleeping like a top
Doesn't get up before noon, no way
I'm used to making bed round him
But got a shock when I threw back duvet

He didn't move, he just snored on
I were about to apprehend
When I noticed that my HRT patch
Were stuck on his rear end

I debated should I tell him
Whether or not to say
Then I thought, no let *him* find out
It won't be long before he goes out to play

I'll tell you what I had to smile
He sneaked across to number four
I thought, it won't be long before she finds out
Just what we went to doctors for

He weren't very long before he came home
Looking flustered, cheeks a bit red
'I expect you'll be taking it off,' I said
'And sticking it back somewhere in bed'

'And if I were you I'd start worrying
Female hormones aren't good for men
You might be neither use nor ornament
When you nip over road again'

LOOSE TEETH AND WOMEN

Doris is having a bit of trouble
With her dentures, the bottom set
She said. 'Somehow, they don't feel just right
I'm really beginning to fret'

'They're getting so uncomfortable
And my gums are getting sore
I'm having a problem cracking nuts
It's starting to be a chore'

I said. 'Eh love, your face it's all screwed up
Don't go putting up with it
Get yourself down to dentists and
Ask him to check the fit'

When I rang to make th'appointment
They said she hadn't been for years
I said. 'Don't worry, Doris I'll come with you
It'll help to calm your fears'

Well we got there Wednesday afternoon
And we sat in t'waiting room
Terrible pictures of teeth on the walls
Place were all doom and gloom

Only one goldfish in the tank
Magazines were all out of date
Suddenly a masked woman appeared
Bellowing, *Mrs. Rawbottom - you're late*

Doris said. 'Elsie, come in with me
Sit in corner over there
I don't fancy being left alone
With that dentist and his chair'

'I remember last time our Nellie came
'Course hers weren't in right good nick
I don't want to end up suffering like her
Having to have a big prick'

He sat her down and tipped her up
'Open wide, Mrs. Rawbottom,' he said
'There's something sadly wrong with these
They're not right size for your head'

'I don't think these can possibly be yours
It's no wonder that they hurt
It's not surprising that you've had to come
Are you sure they're not your Bert's?'

Doris said, 'I don't understand
They were on my side on t'bedroom floor
I always put 'em in that glass
No!! Not her from number four?'

She looked at me and tried to speak
Not easy, when your worlds upside down
She said. 'I'll bet it were a week last Tuesday
When we both went into town'

'And thinking about my problem
They haven't felt right since then
Well there's no way *I'm* taking them back to her
You'll have to ask your Len'

'And neither do I want mine back
Let her wear 'em, or at least let her try
And my Bert can buy me some new ones
The best that money can buy'

SEASONAL GREETINGS

Dumplings on T' Menu
Big Turkeys and Small Parcels
A Right Old Pantomime
The Christmas Fairy
Flash Bang Wallop

DUMPLINGS ON T' MENU

Do you know what we did last weekend?
Went to Bert's annual works do
Dinner and Dance in a nice hotel
Pity we'd to take them two

We'd saved up and been to January Sales
For shoes and a nice cocktail frock
We found sparkly beads on t'market
And two bags in real mock croc

Bert and Leonard wore their old D.J's
I said. 'Doris they look a bit tricky
Every one's going to be staring at them
Look at size of your Lens dicky'

We decided to go in Len's Reliant
He said he weren't going to drink
'Doris' I said. 'We've heard it all before
We'll take our bus fare, I think'

We went straight to Powder Room when
we got there
Lovely plants and pot pourri on a shelf
There were a china saucer full of small change
I think you can just help yourself

Well we got sat down at the table
It were right on th'edge of dance floor
And who should be sat across from us
But that floozy from number four

I looked at Doris; she shook her head
And whispered, 'Them two are in for a treat
Have you seen how far down that neckline is
You can nearly see her feet'

'Looks like there's dumplings on t'menu'
Said Bert, with a gleam in his eye
I said. 'There might be, but you're
not having 'em
So don't think you can try'

Well meal turned out to be quite nice
Prawns, chicken, then lemon mousse
Then the band struck up a Gay Gordons
And them two were out on t'loose

Jackets came off; shirt necks were undone
As they twirled number four 'cross the floor
I said. 'Doris let's leave 'em to it
But we're bolting that front door'

So we got our coats and changed our shoes
And caught the last bus home
We went on top deck, sat at the back
And had a right good moan

About work and life and family
But mostly about Bert and Len
So we've decided if we go next year
We'll not take them two again

BIG TURKEYS AND SMALL PARCELS

What sort of Christmas did you have last year
Ours were pretty grim
We ended up shopping with them two
It's trying to fit everything in

We'd had to take them with us
To carry all food and drink
This year we'll do it different
We'll order on t'internet I think

We'd all stuff to unload in kitchen
Piled up all over the floor
Fridge were stuffed to capacity
We couldn't shut bloomin' door

Bert said they'd find somewhere for bottles
So they put 'em in garden shed
'Course we never saw them rest a day
Eight o'clock they were flat out in bed

Well Christmas Eve we'd loads to do
And them two have hangovers from hell
So we got 'em peeling vegetables
Then stuffing turkey as well

You should have seen the size of it
It must have been thirty two pound
I said, 'Why have they got such a big one
There's far too much to go round'

'Course it didn't fit in th'oven
And we wanted it to roast overnight
'Len,' I said, 'Chop it's legs off'
Even then it were still a bit tight

Well we went to bed after midnight
Exhausted we dropped off straight away
Me and Doris need our beauty sleep
There were fourteen for dinner next day

They were all due around about eleven
So we left present opening 'til then
We'd no idea what we were getting
But it'll be a surprise from Bert and Len

We couldn't wait to get 'em opened
I must say they were gift wrapped well
We like to squeeze and guess just
what they are
But we were really struggling to tell

Well we don't normally get small parcels
It's usually summat for kitchen instead
But this time we got the shock of our lives
Undies, all flimsy and red

'So you reckon these'll suit us?'
Bert couldn't look me in the eye
'We hope you'll like 'em,' he stammered
'We weren't right sure what to buy'

'Right,' I said to Doris
'Now all relations have gone
Let's nip upstairs to bedroom
Then we can try 'em on'

I'd just managed to squeeze into 'em
When someone knocked at door
Them two were asleep, so I had to go
Well it were her from number four

She looked at us and started to laugh
'You should be careful you'll get
yourselves banned
And I think these might be yours,' she said
She'd a chip pan in either hand

Well I can tell you we weren't speaking
Not to them two, we gave em sack
On bright side we did need new chip pans
But flimsy red undies went back

A RIGHT OLD PANTOMIME

They've been auditioning for Christmas Panto
It's Cinderella this year
It's being put on in Village Hall
Well it's handy, we live quite near

Me and Elsie know the parts we're suited too
I don't know why other folks bother
Elsie'll makes a lovely Cinders
And I'll be her fairy godmother

Len has dug up his prize pumpkin
He said. 'This is one of me best
A bit of magic and it's a fairy coach
That'll put prop department to test'

Bert brought along some ferrets
He were sorry, but he couldn't catch mice
'Wave a wand over these four' he said
'And you'll have ponies in a trice'

Course Len thinks he should be
Prince Charming
Dressed up in hose and satin keks
But there's not an ounce of charm about him
And anyroad, he's wrong sex

Bert fancies his chances as Buttons
He's undone quite a few in his time
He'll get plenty of practice this Christmas
And most of 'em won't be mine

Well queue seemed to go on forever
It went well past Village Hall door
Elsie said. 'Have you seen whose behind us
That slapper from number four'

'Well that one ugly sister, sorted', I said
'I wonder whose going to be second?'
I could see producer eyeing us up
Then he crooked his finger and beckoned

'Right ladies, don't move a muscle' he said
Looking us up and down from heads to our feet
'You two won't be needing much make up
In fact all the requirements, you meet'

We left Village Hall walking on air
I said. 'Elsie we must have been best
He were obviously very impressed with us
We were far better than the rest'

He gave us scripts to read through
We were starting rehearsals next day
And we couldn't wait to get started
It looked like we'd a lot to say

I said. 'Wait a minute, this isn't right
There's no mention here of me wand
In fact he hasn't given us the starring rolls
I reckon we've been conned'

Well you can guess who were Cinderella
You're right that two timing flirt
And yes, Leonard been cast as Buttons
And Prince Charming, you've guessed it,
were Bert

'Prince Charming and Buttons! Elsie' I said
Prince Charming's a girl, not a mister
Just then the producer shouted out loud
'Could I have the two ugly sisters'

'Elsie he seems to be pointing at us
The whole things a bloomin' disgrace
Mind you the sight of them two in tights
Should soon wipe that smile of *her* face.'

But on the night o'performance
We can guarantee Cinderella'll frown
'Cos me and Elsie have been down
t'joke shop
And put itching powder in her ballgown.

THE CHRISTMAS FAIRY

They've been auditioning for
Christmas Santas
So we sent them two along
I said. 'Both of you had better get
washed and shaved
And change them trousers, they don't half pong'

They got in queue quite early
It were a bit like pop idol on t'telly
They needed two jolly gentlemen
With red faces and big bellies

Both of 'em fit the bill nicely
They eat and drink a lot you see
Which causes flushing and a beer gut
We find it disgusting Doris and me

Of course the job it tends to be seasonal
In fact it's only three weeks at the most
And the grottos in the centre of Blackburn
That's where they'd take up their post

Well they came home yo- ho- ho-ing
The job if they wanted it were theirs
It worked out just right apparently
As they'd wanted men in pairs

They'd do two shifts between 'em
One in, whilst the other has tea
Bert said. 'They say the job can be stressful
Having to bounce children on your knee'

The costumes arrived on Friday
Red suit, black wellies, a white beard
And when they tried them on for us
They didn't look as bad as we'd feared

They started work this Saturday
The grotto was all-aglow
With lights and tinsel and Christmas trees
And a ton and a half of fake snow

The little ones had formed an orderly queue
So we stepped in behind
I said. 'Doris I can't wait to see 'em both
Goodness knows just what we'll find'

Leonard were having his cuppa
So my Bert were in Santa's chair
Doris nudged me in the ribs, and asked
'Have you seen whose over there?'

There she stood, magic wand in hand
White tutu, stood on tip - toe
Dumplings were hanging over top of it
And varicose veins were on show

'Quick duck down behind
this Christmas tree
She hasn't seen us yet'
I said. 'Doris she'll be in cahoots with them
They'll be up to no good, you can bet'

Just then a little lad ran out crying
'Mummy he weren't bothered about me
I only wanted to talk to Santa
But there's a great big fairy sat in there
on his knee'

FLASH BANG WALLOP

Everybody's doing it this Christmas
Decorating up on th'outside
It brightens up the whole of the street
And you can look at it with pride

So we sent them two off to B and Q
And garden centre on t' way back
Good job Len's Robin Reliant
Has a fairly big roof rack

As usual they were missing for ages
We were wondering just where they were
When we heard this cursing and swearing
As they pulled up with a seven foot fir

They started unloading Reliant
I said. 'Have you got it all here?'
'No, there's a van delivering tomorrow
A nine foot snowman, a sledge and reindeer'

Well there were hundreds of bulbs on wires
Little elves with fibre optics inside
I said. 'Where on earth is it all gonna go
Front garden's only twelve foot wide?'

Bert said, 'I hope you're not going out
tomorrow
'Cos that van'll be coming you know
With all that stuff we've ordered
And four and a half tons of fake snow'

'Snowman can stand in front garden
With fairy lights draped all around
Reindeer and sledge can go up on t'roof
Providing we can get 'em off ground'

'There's also a musical Santa
Plays Jingle Bells all of the time'
I said. 'Bert don't you think it's all a bit much?'
He said. 'Stop worrying it'll all be just fine'

Well they've never been good at erections
And this job were proving a big task
I said. 'Elsie where on earth is it going to go
She said. 'Eh love I'd rather not ask'

I must say it caused lots of interest
Children stood round front door
Then she came across being nosy
Christmas Fairy from number four

'Well they seem to be doing a right good job
I like way Bert's decorated that pine
Then she winked at him quite blatantly
And asked. 'When you coming to do mine?'

I said, 'He won't be coming across at all
So don't go thinking he will
And since you're house'll have a
front row seat
How do you feel about sharing the bill?'

We couldn't wait for half past seven
All neighbours were going to come out
Ready to witness the switch on
They were bound to cheer an shout

They all counted to ten, Bert pulled the switch
I said. 'Elsie how's this for a lark?'
There were an almighty flash bang wallop
And bloomin' street lamps went dark

They'd wired everything up to street lamps
Talk about overload
Now street lighting departments sent
an almighty bill
For repairing every lamp in road

HAPPY NEW YEAR

Bowlers and Basques
Another Year Older and Deeper in Debt

BOWLERS AND BASQUES

Bert did look a mess in his trousers
Doris asked. 'Don't you think
they're a bit tight
Didn't they have a bigger size?
He doesn't half look a fright'

Bert were dressing up as Scrooge
Len, the ghost of Christmas past
I'd hired this Cleopatra frock
Complete with rubber asp

We'd decided to throw a party
As last New Years Eve what a mess!
We were going to have it at our house
With optional fancy dress

We'd invited all the neighbours
Our Nellie and her Fred
Doris were going as Carmen Miranda
Wi' fruit bowl strapped on her head

Mind you we hadn't invited you know who
Not with our Len and Bert
You see we've made this resolution
To get rid of the two timing flirt

We'd done lots of Horses Doovers
Beef paste butties, not too thick
A barrel of beer and sweet sherry
And twiddly bits on sticks

Our Nellie arrived at 9.30
With inebriated Fred
They were dressed as Laurel and Hardy
Black bowler hats on their head

'I'm sorry we're late' said Nellie
'He's like this every New Year
I thought all your neighbours were coming
Are we the only ones here?'

'Ish that young woman coming?'
He'd had enough had our Fred
'Her as like the fellas'
'No, she's not coming' I said.

Ten o'clock came, then eleven
Nobody had turned up at all
Bert Len and Fred had had too much
They all looked ready to fall

Big Ben were striking midnight
There came a hammering at front door
'Better late than never, here they all come'
But no, it were her from number four

'I've come to bring New Year in' she said
Heels so high she could hardly stand
Wobbling in basque and suspenders
A piece of coal in her hand

'Happy New Year' she shouted
'My the sights you see when you
haven't your gun
My party's tarts and vicars
And we aren't half having fun'

'You can all come across if you want to'
I said. 'No, we'll leave them three asleep
New Years Eve *we* could do with a laugh
Men are enough to make you weep'

We found where neighbours had got to
Everyone were up and having a dance
Me and Doris soon joined in
It's not often we get the chance

Later on I crept into the kitchen
I didn't make much sound
There were our Nellie kissing a vicar
And she'd turned his collar wrong way round

So here we all are day after
Start of a new year and them two feel sick
But there's Horses Doovers for breakfast
And beef paste butties, not too thick

ANOTHER YEAR OLDER AND DEEPER IN DEBT

'New Years Eve' Bert said. 'Are we
going out?'
I said. 'Not if it's like last year
Us two catching last bus home
You two, full of beer'

'Oh come on Elsie' said Doris
We're not spending New Year at home'
'Well I'm not going with them two ' I said
'Right then, we'll go on our own'

Well I can tell you they pulled their faces
Our suggestion fell quite flat
'And just where do you reckon
two women can go
On their own, when they're fifty plus VAT?'

Well that did it. 'We're using Reliant' I said
'Get your make up, high heels and best frock
I've heard of this club in Regent St
Apparently the whole place rocks'

We wandered round 'til we found it
This club called Jazzy Kex
The man on the door shook his head at us
'Go on then, it's New Year, what the heck'

It weren't half dark when we got inside
Music that loud – you couldn't think
We elbowed our way to the front of the bar
'Excuse me, we need a big drink'

This nice young woman approached us
'Now what would you two ladies like?'
'Just mix us a cocktail' said Doris
'A big 'un, it is New Years night'

Four drinks later my arms had no feeling
And Doris had started to sway
'I fancy shaking a leg,' she cried
'Just point me in the right way'

A young fella were sat in this corner
He didn't stand a chance
He protested. 'I'm waiting for girlfriend'
'No you're not, we're having a dance'

Sight of Doris and him up and dancing
I've not seen her like it for years
Gyrating and bending, flailing her arms
Just watching her fair brought on tears

All of a sudden she staggered
A handbag hit her square on the jaw
'He's mine take your hands off him grandma
We're getting married next week don't you
know'

We were escorted out by the bouncer
Blond girl behind bar waved goodbye
'Let's go home' I said. 'We've had enough
In t'morning you'll have a black eye'

When we got back to Reliant we'd a ticket
Illegal parking; I said, 'I feel sick'
She said. 'You will be, wheels are all missing
They've left it propped up on three bricks'

We sat in taxi going home
A year older and deeper in debt
'What are we going to tell Bert and Len
That's been worse New Years Eve
we've had yet'

MEMORIES AND MEN

Childhood Memories
The Big Freeze
Men

CHILDHOOD MEMORIES

We've been looking back over
the past fifty years
That's only as far as we go
But how things have changed in our lifetime
And not all for the better you know

Remember getting up Winter mornings
Scraping the frost from the pane
Peeping out through the hole you'd made
To see it snowing again

We snuggled back under the eiderdown
To wait for the fire to be lit
Then Mum shouted up, 'Porridge is ready'
And we'd go and huddle round it

Our clothes were in the top oven
Put there to keep warm by Mum
We got dressed quickly in front of t' fire
But there was always a draft round your bum

We'd liberty bodices with rubber buttons
And knee socks that always sag
And round our necks in the Winter
We wore a camphor bag

Before going out every morning
We'd a spoonful of cod liver oil
An important part of our diet
Before the daily toil

Of course in Summer it was different
The sun always seemed to shine more
The children could play out after tea
As the neighbours sat by their door

When we broke up from school we'd go fishing
For tiddlers and newts down at t'cut
Throwing sticks and stones in the water
We took bottles of water and a jam but

Do you remember drawing a hopscotch
And skipping with an old washing line
We used to get ten or twelve in the rope
All jumping together in time

We often played at two ball
Some of us could juggle three
But we would rather play tig with the boys
We were fast cats Doris and me

We always seemed to be scrapping
Or falling and grazing our knee
Run all the way home, hot and sweating
Then Mum sent us out to get tea

We'd grumble all way to Chippy
They'd put basin on range to keep hot
We'd get fish, chips, gravy and a
pile of mushy peas
It took a big basinful to feed us lot

Of course we'd no television
So sat listening to wireless after tea
When we went to bed we couldn't sleep
We'd been listening to Dick Barton, you see

'What's on the table Mabel'
Said Wilfred Pickles on Have a Go
Not forgetting Mrs Dales Diary
And the Life with the Lyons Show

Bedtime always came to early
Tin bath were dragged in from t' yard
We'd to get in it one after t'other
Then Mum would scrub us real hard

So finally to bed with Ovaltine
Our recollections are still sharp and clear
Of the safe and loving childhood we had
These memories to us we hold dear

THE BIG FREEZE

December twenty second, nineteen sixty two
Winter; bad weather, expected it's true
But temperatures plunged, as colder it grew
By gum it were bitterly cold

Snow came down late on Christmas Day
Great for the kiddies, who love to play
But how we wished it would go away
By gum it were awfully cold

Ice crystals covered the window pane
You had to scrape it off again
Tomorrow you knew it'd be the same
By gum it were unbelievably cold

All the pipes were frozen up
Water iced up in the cup
Warm in bed – didn't want to get up
By gum it were terribly cold

By January twentieth we were all snowed in
Dig your way down to the bin
We started to worry about old Uncle Jim
By gum it were frighteningly cold

January twenty fourth, the coldest night
Twenty degrees of frost, cold all right
It didn't improve when it came daylight
By gum it were miserably cold

February came and pipes had burst
Standpipes in street, but that's not worst
Gas pipes fractured, folk started to curse
By gum it were dreadfully cold

Not since eighteen seventy eight had
temperatures been
So cold in February, frost so keen
It might have looked pretty, that snowy scene
But by gum it were numbingly cold

No football for weeks, they changed the rules
A panel decided the football pools
That sort of gambling were only for fools
By gum it were horribly cold

The severe weather made many folk ill
Several old ones, it were known to kill
That dreadful winter we remember still
By gum it were despairingly cold

But the frost at last began to go
As March came in, it began to thaw
Daffodils peeping through the snow
By gum the sun felt warm

MEN!!!!

Dirty crockery in the sink
Underneath, an awful stink
Waste bin hasn't been emptied, I think
For at least a couple of weeks

Unmade bed, wrinkled sheets
Drawers left open in t'bedroom suite
I hold me hand up; admit defeat
There are clothes all over the floor

Empty bottles, you know the score
Glasses and cans all over the floor
Picking 'em up would be such a chore
Men can't bend down, you see

Dirty ring around the rim
Must have filled the bath t'brim
Obviously couldn't find the Vim
Has he been down pit?

Washing basket overflows
Just what's in there, heaven knows
I think there's more than dirty clothes
I really dread to think

Fat in chip pan's gone quite hard
Must have used two pound o' lard
But why's he left it out in t'yard?
He must have had a fire

Cooker's in a terrible mess
Covered in grease, more or less
He tells me he's had a lot of stress
Cooking for himself

Well I'd better go and empty bin
But I've got to say I'll never win
Is it worth it going on holiday, again
And leaving *him* at home?

A BIT MORE BESIDES

Wish You Were Here
Foundations and Bunny Rabbits
Net Curtains and Uranus
Pleasure Cruises and Chip Shops
Brass Bands and Swingers
Strawberries and Sagging Sofas
Glossy Photographs and Vests

Wish you Were Here...

Dear Doris

Well here we are, it does seem funny not having you and Len with us but I'll have to grit my teeth, grin and bear it. The weather's very breezy and it hasn't stopped raining since we got here. Lodgings seem to be OK; we've got a nice double room with a wash basin, bathrooms not too far down the hall. Oh and there's a trouser press in the room, well I think that what it is, mind you I dare say it'll not get much use. And before you go thinking the worst we've got twin beds, they've got lovely candlewick bedspreads, they don't exactly match, but they are a similar sort of pink. Curtains are pink as well; though they don't shut properly, window looks over backyard and dustbins, but do you know Doris even though we're facing away from prom you still get a glow from illuminations. Landlady seems nice enough, she's given us a key, but says we have to be in for eleven or else she'll put sneck down. Well I'd best finish, its time to get changed for us tea. Write if you can,

Love Elsie.

Dear Elsie

Good to hear you've got a nice place. I still can't believe you and Bert have gone away on your own. What on earth are you going to talk about and it might be twin beds, but I don't like the sound of them at all, why go courting bother? Remember what happened when we went on that coach trip to Cleethorpes, how embarrassed you were having to go down to reception and tell them one bed had collapsed when you tried to pull 'em apart. You're better off when we come, so us two can share and them two can be in another room of their own. Still never mind it'll soon pass, it's only ten days, it could be worse. Keep smiling,

Love Doris.

Dear Doris

We've just finished breakfast, so I thought I'd drop you a line. Supposed to be full English, but you only get a choice of cereal and then you get what you're given. Today it were boiled egg, I got one, but she gave Bert two. 'She' being the landlady's daughter, about forty I'd say, bleached blond, top heavy, you know the type, well you should we've one across the street. Well as she were putting his two eggs in front of him she sort of leant over and being kind of top heavy, collided with Bert's bald patch. 'Enjoy your breakfast sir.' she says. Oh he enjoyed it alright and I saw him wink at her as we were going out of dining room. I'm going to make sure he sits with his back to the wall tomorrow so she can't get behind him. They never give up do they? Well wind seems to have dropped and I think it's stopped raining so we're going for a walk down Golden Mile.

Hope all is well with you,

Love Elsie.

Dear Elsie

I'm sorry to hear about the landlady's daughter, her sort are always bad news. And speaking of bad news Elsie, you've had a flood. I went in to check that everything was alright and it wasn't, there were water dripping through kitchen ceiling. I went upstairs into bathroom and Bert must have left tap running in washbasin and your Blacky must have jumped in it, I don't know how he must have wanted a drink, anyway he'd blocked plug hole and basin had overflowed, so there's water everywhere. Anyroad I turned tap off and I've cleaned up best I could. So it's not too bad, so don't go worrying Elsie. Oh did I mention cat were dead, I weren't sure what to do, so I've dried it off best I could with your hairdryer and I've put it in your shed. I thought you might like some sort of a ceremony seeing you've had it so long. Not that I like tom cats, their habits are too near home for my liking. I keep watching weather forecast, I see it's still unsettled, well never mind,
All for now,

Love Doris

Dear Doris

Thank goodness you were there. What would I do without you? I could kill Bert and now he tells me he's let insurance lapse. I tell you if you don't do it yourself it doesn't get done, still there's no point bothering I'll sort it out when I come home. Thank you for telling me cat's dead, but it's not ours, I took our Blacky to cattery, so I'm a bit mystified to say the least. There you go again, if Bert had blocked cat flap up like I told him to do this wouldn't have happened. Anyroad leave it in shed 'til I get back. On a brighter note I went to Bingo last night and won six sticks of rock, so I'll share them with you when I get back. Bert went to pictures, some war film or other, I hate war films, there's enough fighting in everyday life that's what I always say. It were late though when he got in it must have been a long film. I were nearly asleep, I'm sure it were past eleven, but he must have got in somehow. Funny thing at breakfast this morning though, I'm sure she muttered something under her breath about firing blanks when she were giving him his one sausage and one rasher of bacon, for once he'd only got same as I had. Maybe she's been to see the same film. He did seem a bit down in the mouth though; I couldn't get a peep out of him. I wonder if she'd got in trouble with her mother for giving him too much breakfast. Anyway enough of that, guess what? I'm going to get my palm read today; I wonder what she will tell me?

Hope it's going to be good,

Love Elsie.

Dear Elsie

I look forward to sharing some of your winnings, you are kind, but oh! Elsie I have to say this, I am surprised at you, with all the experience you've had of other women and you haven't cottoned on. Bert's obviously been up to no good while you were playing bingo. War films indeed, if you ask me, he hadn't earned his extra sausage and bacon, well that's how I see it, we've always been honest with one another Elsie and I hope I haven't upset you. Oh! and speaking of other women, the slapper from across road were out early this morning shouting 'puss, puss, puss' all over the street. Lost her precious Persian, says it a black one, she knocked our door and asked if Len could give her a hand looking for the thing. Naturally I didn't say anything, but I told her Len were too busy. No wonder it blocked plug- hole all that fur and it did take a such long time to dry off. I don't know what to do Elsie? We'll decide when you get back.

Only a few days to go and I see it still raining

Chin up,

Love Doris.

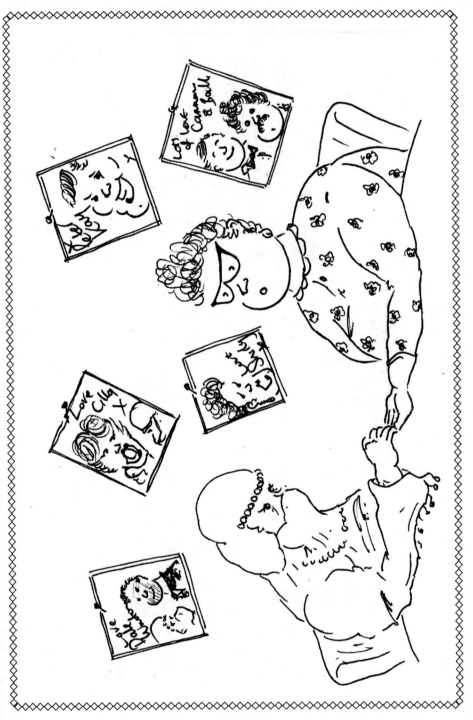

Dear Doris

It's poured down all night and I couldn't sleep, I reckon you were right about landlady's daughter she's feeding some other fella up now with extra portions. Bert seems to have recovered though. He bought himself a "Kiss me Quick" hat so I think you can say hope springs eternal, no doubt he'll be going across to number four in it when we get back. Fancy it being her cat! I didn't know she had one, we'll get rid of it as soon as we can, don't let on to her though or she'll never be off our backs. Eh! I went to have me palm read, Gypsy Petrulengo, she's really good. She told me I'm not in a happy marriage, my husband is a lazy good for nothing and I'm plagued with other women, she were spot on, then she said I would be coming into money and going across the ocean and chances were I'd might meet a tall dark stranger, sooner rather than later. She were right about that, Bert got arrested last night; a tall dark stranger in a policeman's helmet brought him back to lodgings. I'd stopped in, I wanted to watch Coronation Street in television lounge and he'd gone out for just one pint, or so he said. He'd been in Yates Wine Lodge, and got arguing with a Blackburn supporter about Accrington Stanley and he'd ended up pouring his drink over him. He'd had a lot more than one I can tell you, they cautioned him and said next time there'd be a fine. Oh I am ready to come home, three more days to go, I can't wait, we'll be home just after six, get me some bread and milk will you.

See you soon,

Love Elsie.

Dear Elsie

I hope you get this before you leave; I've been back in and kept checking your house. It seems to have dried up all right. There's not too much damage, kitchen wallpapers come loose and you need some new oilcloth down in there, but its not too bad at all, it could have been a lot worse. Funny carry on though. Len, decided to get off his backside for once and do summat, said he'd mow that patch of grass out front for you, it hadn't half grown probably due to all rain we've had. Well he went to shed for your mower and next news I hear him shouting for me over back yard wall. 'Doris, come here quick cats gone.' Well, I rushed round and there it were gone! I tell you Elsie it were as dead as a door nail, when I left it there, or at least I could have sworn it was. It fair put me off me tea and Len said he couldn't face cutting your grass after a shock like that, so I'm sorry Elsie, Bert'll have to do it when you get home. I thought well, I need to get to bottom of this, so I forced myself to go across road to number four's. I were just raising me hand to knock on her front door when I noticed bloomin cat inside, sat on window sill asleep. 'Course she spotted me and come straight to door. 'What do you want?' she sez and as she said it the flipping thing jumped down and shot out between my legs and what's more Elsie it looked like it were having kittens to me. I didn't wait to answer her; I just scuttled back across road sharpish. I don't know what to say, it will just have to remain one of life's little mysteries, least said soonest mended. Anyroad I nipped down to Co-op and your bread and milk's in larder, Len says he'll meet you at the station in Reliant if you let us know what time, so you don't have to carry your cases on bus. I can't wait to see you; I'll be across just as soon as you get back,
I expect we'll have a lot to tell one another.
See you Saturday,

Love Doris

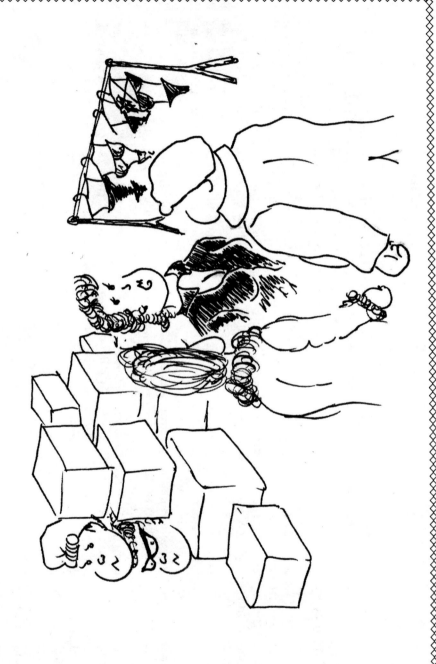

FOUNDATIONS AND BUNNY RABBITS

I said 'Elsie look at the state of me
I'm feeling right down in the mouth
Even my Len has mentioned
That every things moving down south'

'We'll go to Blackburn on Tuesday
I need a firm foundation for me
Anyroad elastics gone in these old ones
Me stocking keep falling round .knee'

She said. 'We'll try Debenham's and Mark's'
But they'd nowt substantial on show
'We need a proper corset shop,' I said
'I know just where to go'

She said. 'It all looks a bit flimsy in window
But we'll look inside just in case
Eh Elsie I'm not so sure about this
It seems to be all black and red lace'

There were a young woman stood behind counter
Pretty girl dressed all in black
Not many other customers
Just a fella in a hat and a mac

'Can I help you ladies?'
'A corset with suspenders,' I said
'Larger sizes are all down here
We've got this lovely number in red'

Elsie looked all hot and bothered
'I can't squeeze me body in that
I need a panty girdle or a corset
Something to contain all me fat'

'Well we don't really have that sort of thing
But you're welcome to look around'
'Eh Doris, come and have a look at this'
I couldn't believe what she'd found

At back of the shop up a corner
Were boxes stacked up on a shelf
Some very funny looking objects
And a sign saying "Do it Yourself"

I said. 'Hang on a minute Elsie'
As I picked up this odd looking thing
'It looks just like a little pink rabbit
With a carrot on a piece of string'

'Eee Elsie I said, look, behind the counter
That's a big one do you think I should I ask'
'Sorry love, that's not for sale
That's me half pint tartan flask'

At that moment shop door opened
And guess who sauntered inside
Done up like an old dogs dinner
I said. 'Elsie quick lets hide'

We hid behind some boxes
As she wiggled to the back of the shop
She said. 'I'm sorry I'm late' then she saw us
But it were a bit too late to stop

The odd looking man in the raincoat
Turned round to her and started to flirt
He were holding black fluffy handcuffs
Under that hat were my Bert

'And what are you doing here?' I screamed
'About the same as you two no doubt'
'Well we came to buy a foundation
And we're not going home wi' nowt'

We left the trollop buying fishnets tights
And took Bert home with us
We all went home in Reliant
Number four had to catch the bus

I said. 'Never mind Elsie who needs men?
You bought something far better instead'
She got the DIY manual and that rabbit
Something really worth taking to bed

NET CURTAINS AND URANUS

You know how Bert and Len like their hobbies
They've had so many in the past
There's always summat fishy
And they never seem to last

Well the latest craze for our two
Something they haven't done before
Involved a telescope and binoculars
And shutting bedroom door.

Around ten thirty every evening
They'd both disappear upstairs
We can hear 'em thumping and banging
They have to do everything in pairs

'Just what are they doing?' asked Elsie
'Let's go and listen at door
I think Bert's saying poke it 'outta window
Make sure it's stands level on floor'

'I don't like sound of this,' I said
'Go down to kitchen and get us a glass
We need to know just what they're on about
I don't think we should let it pass'

Elsie pressed glass up against the bedroom door
'I can hear 'em clearly,' she said
'And whatever it is their doing
I reckon they've moved the bed'

Len's saying, 'Over there that's Uranus
And look you can see the Great Bear
In the sky quite close together
To see 'em like that is quite rare'

'Now Bert saying summat about mooning
What a great sight to behold
He's asking Len if he's seen Virgo rising
And how small things look when they're cold.'

'I've had enough of this,' I said. 'Elsie
Give 'em a knock on the door'
'You can't come in,' shouted Leonard
'There's stuff all over the floor'

'Open this door this instant
Or else we'll batter it down
Where on earth has that spy glass come from?'
Asked Elsie with a frown

'We've taken up astronomy
We thought you'd both be impressed'
'So you're keeping a close eye on t'fourth galaxy
By watching her get undressed'

And across the road at number four
The lacy net curtains were drawn
And silhouetted with the light behind
Were her doing a strip on her own.

'And how long as this been goin' on?
'We're only watching the sky at night'
Bert stammered.. 'Honest we'd only just noticed her
She gave us such a fright'.

'Right well now you've both spotted Venus
You can take your telescope down
Tomorrow it goes in Reliant
And you take it to Pawn Shop up town'

PLEASURE CRUISES AND CHIP SHOPS

It had seemed a good idea
Walking ten miles along canal
Clayton le Moors to Burnley
We were doing it with this pal

Lily, she works in George's Chippy
Needs exercise, wants to get trim
But with all the steak pudding and chips she eats
She makes me and Doris look thin

We set off bright and early
To register for the walk
I were beginning to wish we'd left Lily behind
She does nothing else but talk

Course Bert and Len didn't want to come
Though we're loath to leave 'em at home
But I said to Doris. 'We can check on them
I've brought me mobile phone'

It were a lovely day on towpath
When we'd gone about three mile
There were a stall selling bacon butties
At least it kept Lily quiet for a while

We were doing it to raise some money
We're big on charity you see
Derian House always need funds
And we care do Doris and me

I wished somebody 'ud gag Lily
She hasn't shut up proper for miles
We've had her prolapse, her false teeth and her
husband
Her bunions and her piles

I looked at Doris she'd turned bright red
Her poor face it said it all
She moaned. 'I shouldn't have worn me new
corsets
Not on this long haul'

We'd reached about the half way mark
And going had started to get rough
I said. 'We could leave the towpath further down
I reckon we've' done enough'

Lily chipped in mid sentence
She said. 'Why don't we hitch a ride
There's plenty of canal boats sailing past
One could soon pull into the side'

I said. 'And who do you think'll stop for us
Where's me mobile I'll ring Bert and Len
They can collect us in Reliant
We'll just have to hutch up again'

'I'll ask him to set off straight away
I reckon they could get here quite soon
Eh up that's odd, I can hear Bert's phone
ringing
It has such a distinctive tune'

'It's coming from that boat over there'
Said Lily. 'What the heck
And isn't that your neighbour
Sunning herself on deck?'

And peeping through barge windows
Guiltily were Bert and Len
And on barge side it read "Fancy a Pleasure
Cruise?"
Them two were at it again.

'Right you two steer it into side'
Angrily I screamed into phone
'Come on Doris and Lily
We're getting a lift back home'

We're not speaking to our two for a while
But Lily needs no encouragement to be lippy
She doesn't half have a tale to tell
To everyone in George's chippy

BRASSBANDS AND SWINGERS

You just wouldn't believe their latest venture
But it involves a lot of hot air
They've only gone and joined this 'ere brass
band
Well they've plenty of wind to be fair

My Len's always blown his own trumpet
So he thought he'd give a real one a go
And Bert said he fancied trying French horn
There's summat behind it though

They've been practising for more than two
months now
Blowing with all of their might
Me and Elsie can't stand the racket
They're at it morning and night

They're trying to master this tongue-ing
We can't understand all the fuss
I tell you me and Elsie weren't to pleased at all
When they asked could they practice on us

Band leader said they were overdoing things
Said he thought they looked a bit rough
With their faces all red and swollen
Maybe they hadn't enough puff

'We're not taking no for an answer
Nothings ever beaten us yet'
Said Bert, hands lovingly round his horn
As Leonard fingered his trum-pet

Well it got they were going most evenings
Len said 'Practice makes perfect you know
If we fail to master these instruments
We'll be given summat to bang, not blow'

We decided we should support them
So we went down to club one night
I said 'Elsie there's women going in as well
Something doesn't feel right'

And guess who had their hand up a cornet
Red in face givin' it a good blow
Bert and Len sat either side
Trying to put on a good show

And she had proper uniform on
Purple jacket short tight black skirt
It's obviously it's not her first visit here
In her six inch heels, the flirt

Well we've just about had enough
And revenge eaten cold can be sweet
So we've decided to join this jazz band
There's an advert in phone box down street

They're looking for women who know how
to swing
It sounds interesting I'm sure you'll agree
We know how to shake our tambourines
So we're going to ring number and see.

STRAWBERRIES AND SAGGING SOFAS

'Self sufficiency's all the rage'
My Bert said, looking smug
'This year we're going to start growin' things
Me and Len have caught the bug'

'We've decided to go organic
It's a great idea we've got
We saw your Fred down Red Lion
And he's givin' up his plot'

'So we thought we might take it over
Organic vegetables are all the rage
And you like your herbs and spices
We can grow rosemary, mint and sage'

I went round to have a word with Doris
'Shop bought veg *is* second best'
At least this time it's summat useful
I think we should be impressed'.

We didn't see 'em from dawn to dusk
They were coming home exhausted
They said when it were ready we could have a tour
Meanwhile they'd keep us posted

Well it certainly kept 'em busy
And away from her and pub
Bert said soil were turned over and planted
We'd soon have our organic grub

And we could go down with 'em day after
Well I can tell you it were a sight to be seen
We weren't right sure just what it all were
It all looked a bit tangled and green

And there were this natty little garden shed
I remarked to Doris, 'Eee this looks cosy
With that old deckchair and battered kettle
I reckon our future looks rosy'

Well a couple of months went flying by
Then vegetables started arriving
Potatoes, carrots, a few green beans,
Obviously things were thriving

Then one teatime, just at the end of March
They brought these strawberries home
'I don't think you get English strawberries in March' I said
'But then I'm no gastronome'

'I reckon we should go and check it out
Looks like there's summat fishy to me
We'll nip down to plot this afternoon
Before we start making the tea'

It did seem to have overgrown a bit
Weeds all over a flower bed
There were music coming from somewhere
And pink curtains up at shed

Well me and Doris stormed inside
We couldn't believe our eyes
Them two, a record player and a mini fridge
It had all been a pack of lies

There were bottles of wine and lager
The trollop's handbag and her packet of fags
A sagging sofa, but worst of all
A neat pile of Tesco bags

'So this is your idea of gardening
No wonder you've both been keen
And as to them sticky green fingers
I'd like to know, just where they've been'

So t'self sufficiency's gone for a burton
And *she's* seen the last o'that garden shed
Veg is still coming from Tesco
But the plot's gone back to our Fred

GLOSSY PHOTOGRAPHS AND VESTS

It's not good when time catches up with you
And you're feeling down in the mouth
Red veins appearing like road maps
Every thing going down south

Crows feet crinkling around the eyes
With sagging bags below
Jowls hanging like a bulldog's
Youth, seems a long time ago

And her at number four doesn't help
Hanging round Bert and Len
I found this photo in Bert's pocket
Looks like they've been at it again

It were her in flimsy what not
Draped over back o' settee
Tarty red heels and a hairpiece
Showing a lot more than a knee

I said to Doris, 'I refuse to be beat
Let's look on t'internet
We'll have a saucy photo done
Find someone to aid and abet'

Someone who knows what he's doing
Who won't mind us making a fuss
Elsie look, t'Garth Dawson Studio
This here fella's leaping out at us

Eh Doris he looks a bit trendy
Do you think he'll be alright?
Well ring him up we'll soon find out
Get him to take us by candlelight

We spoke to a young woman called Julie
I asked her, 'what do you think we should
wear?
She said. 'It depend what effect you hope to
achieve
I said. 'Well our husbands are having an affair'

We booked appointment for Friday morning
We were fair excited Doris and me
Julie met us in reception
'Would you like a nice cup of tea?'

Reg Whittam
The Garth Dawson Studio
01254 231802

Then Reg came in and sized us up
He asked. 'How do you want to appear?'
I said, 'Well we'd like to look a bit glamorous
So we've brought summat a little bit sheer

'We want the lines erasing
We want to look tall and thin
We want to look twenty years younger'
He asked, 'and is this first studio you've bin?,'

'You realise you will be a challenge
But I always do my best
Now I've got this thing called a beauty dish
I reckon you two'll put it to test'

He had us in all sorts of poses
Every now and again we could rest
Reg said, 'Doris *that* is a nice negligee
But it'd look better minus your vest'

Well we picked photos up last Monday
We couldn't wait to have a look
And if you want to see one
Turn to back cover of our book

And as to Bert and Len's affair
With the floozy at number four
There's a sexy photo of the two of us
Just been pushed through her front door

And finally.......

A few years ago, well quite a few actually, a couple of giggling and girlish ladies burst into Studio 2 at BBC Radio Lancashire. Jim Bowen and I looked at each other; this was going to be fun. Anne Wareing and Kath Eccleston smiled broadly and set about reading their rhymes charting the ups and downs of their alter egos Doris Rawbottom and Elsie Arkwright. Listeners loved them and soon the pair became regular contributors to the show.

So what makes their poetry so popular, I think it's because we can nod our heads and say 'yes that's me; or my other half does that too.' Their writing has gone from strength to strength and I am so chuffed to be asked to write the 'And finally' to what they tell me will possibly be the last of the Doris and Elsie publications.

Anne and Kath have brought us all so many laughs whilst raising so much cash for Derian House with the sales of their books. Thank you girls and for those of you who have just bought and read this book, I bet you enjoyed it and did a bit of nodding too.

Sally Naden
BBC Radio Lancashire